JavaScript
Easy Web Design
With CSS

This book has been tested with several groups of students and received enormous positive responses for its simplicity and enrichment of educational contents.

One of the most important features of this textbook is that all chapters are written by the same author.

Title: JavaScript
   Easy Web Design
Edition: first
Author: Mahmood Shanbedi
Publisher: Nortown Press
www.nortownpress.com

Editor: Matt Snell
Cover Design: Tom Loty
Interior: Lewis Tappa
ISBN: 978-0-9810245-0-9
15 June 2008

This book provides all necessary materials that you needed to master your skills in Web design.
Contact us by e-mail at: info@nortownpress.com

Notice of rights

Preface

This book is nicely divided into two major parts (CSS and JavaScript). The CSS (Cascading Style Sheets) is needed to create very attractive website layout. First you will learn CSS from the beginning in very easy steps then you move to learning JavaScript from the ground up. We assume you have never written a code in CSS or JavaScript, that's why we start from the scratch! Through the learning process you will see the concept of DHTML which is normally combination of HTML, XHTML, CSS and JavaScript. There are plenty of examples, nicely arranged in sequences that make JavaScript easy to understand and easy to code, allowing you to quickly build your website.

Audiences

The book is designed for those who want to learn JavaScript and CSS but they do not have prior skills in scripting languages. The book is suitable for students from "High schools, Colleges, Universities, Individual learning and those who want to build their modern WebPages in short time.

Table of Contents

Part I
CSS

This part of book covers the Cascading Style Sheets (CSS) form the beginning. It provides brief definition along with many examples. We display the graphics result for each example, so students can get some ideas even before running the examples.

Chapter 1

Introduction to CSS

- Introduction
- Formatting Text
- Cascading Style Sheets
- Selector
- Grouping selector
- Inline style
- Class selector
- ID selector
- Group Class Selector
- Font

- Span and div
- Colors
- Four ways to declare RGB
- CSS background
- Background image
- Resize background
- CSS comments
- Review questions
- Answers

Introduction

HTML is easy to learn but unfortunately it does not fulfill all of our demands. We know that some parts of HTML are deprecated; meaning that they are not supported and we should not use them. In this regard, CSS (Cascading Style Sheets) replaces the deprecated features. CSS is a modern way of creating a webpage. It is easy and faster to use. The source code becomes smaller than the regular pure HTML codes. You can design styles once and use it many times. In this chapter you learned some simple features of CSS, especially colors and fonts and then we will look at CSS more thoroughly in this chapter. You must have full knowledge of HTML prior to this point.

Cascading Style Sheets

Cascading Style Sheets or just Style Sheets (widely known as **CSS**) helps you to master your client webpage. It removes some of the weakness of HTML. An advantage of the CSS is that the code becomes significantly shorter. You can create your style inside the head tag and use it for an entire page or pages. You do not need to declare style again and again and, therefore, the code becomes considerably small. To start CSS you need to know the style itself. Style-sheet can be an **internal** or **external** style. The internal style can be body style (entire style) or **Inline** style.

Cascading Style Sheets CSS		
Internal Style	**Body Style**	**Inline style**
	Style for the entire body of the page with the same properties as color, font, background, etc.	Style that is used for *individual lines* inside the code.
External style	Enables us to call an external file of CSS, *filename.css*	

Selector

The selector is the base of CSS. The selector allows you to use your style. The basic selector uses HTML tags like *H1, H2, P, B* and other HTML tags. The general format of selector is:

General Format	Selector	Property	Value
	⇓	⇓	⇓
Example	P	color :	blue

For example you declare property and values like this:

H1 {color: yellow ;}

The **H1** is selector; **color** is a property; **yellow** is a value given to the color property.
Here we will use color and font in CSS then we move to the next section.
We place style inside the head:

```
<Head>
<style type="text/css">
  body { color: blue;  }
</style>
</Head>
```

The selector code must be inside the curly bracket "**{ }**" the **body** is the selector's name and **{ color: blue; }** is the code. The **<style type="text/css">** is telling browser that the CSS code must be parsed. You need to close the style like </**style**> you see the back-slash "/" which means style is closed (end of the style).

HTML and CSS

HTML is all about content and text structures but CSS is about design and layout. In fact we use both along with JavaScript in our modern WebPages. Look at the same code for both.
You can use body background in HTML using this code:

```
<body bgcolor="#FF00FF">
```

We can use CSS style for the same effect.

body {background-color: #FF00FF;}

You can use **multiple properties** like color and background. There can be two or more properties in the same selector such as fonts, colors, background, borders, text formatting and link.

```
<Head>
<style type="text/css">
  body { color: blue;
background: yellow; }
</style>
</Head>
```

Once again, we gave a name "**body**" to our selector which contains two properties: *color* and *background*.

CSS Color and Background properties	
CSS Property	**Description**
color	Text color
background-color	Color of background
background-image	Image attached on background
background-repeat	Multiple background images
background-attachment	Image attachments
background-position	Exact position of image on background
background	Webpage background

This example makes the entire body background yellow with some blue text.
Note: do **NOT** type the numbers beside each line!

Example: 1.1
1. <!DOCTYPE HTML PUBLIC "-//W3C//DTD HTML 4.01//EN"
2. "http://www.w3.org/TR/html4/Strict.dtd">
3. <head>
4. <meta http-equiv="Content-Type" content= "text/html; charset=iso-8859-1">
5. <title> Color and background</title>
6. <**style** type="text/css">
7. body { color: blue; background: yellow; }
8. </**style**> </head>
9. <body> <p>
10. Everything you type here will be in blue!
11. With yellow background!
12. </p> </body>
13. </html>

In the above example, we declared **body {color: blue; background: yellow ;}** inside the head. The *selector's* name is called **body**. Therefore, the entire body of the page will accept the style.

Grouping selector
Selector can be grouped in several tags. For example, you can use it if you want to use different size or styles and so on.
H1, H2, h5, b, I {font-family: Tahoma, Verdana, Arial ;}

Inline style

When you create a style and place it within the head, the entire body of code obeys the pre-set style. What happens if you want to create some new style later? You must change the line of code with a different style (use **inline** style).

`<p style="color: #CCCCCC;">The new formatted text</p>`

Example: 1.2

1. <!DOCTYPE HTML PUBLIC "-//W3C//DTD HTML 4.01//EN"
2. "http://www.w3.org/TR/html4/Strict.dtd">
3. `<head> <meta http-equiv="Content-Type" content="text/html; charset=iso-8859-1">`
4. `<title> Inline Style</title>`
5. **`<style`** `type="text/css">`
6. `b{ font-size: 14pt; color: red; }`
7. **`</style>`** `</head> <body> <p>`
8. `<b>This is a pre-style text in red</b> </p>`
9. **`<H4 style="color: #CCCCCC;" >`** The inline style text in CCCCCC`</H4>`
10. `</body>`
11. `</html>`

You will see that the **inline** style generates different colors. You can use **class** and **ID** in order to do the same thing, which we will learn later.

Fonts

CSS font provides different font-weight: font-style and **font-family**. Just look at this table which shows the different features of files.

Property	Example
font-family	font-family : arial, san-serif
font-size	font-size: normal font-size:10px (size in pixels) font-size:12pt (size in point) **Relative size :** font-size:small font-size:x-small font-size:xx-small font-size:smaller font-size:medium font-size:large font-size:x-large font-size:xx-large font-size:larger font-size:55%

Property	Example
font-style	font-style:normal font-style:italic font-style:oblique
font-weight	font-weight:normal font-weight:bold font-weight:bolder font-weight:lighter **font-weight:100**

- If the font-family is made up of two parts, like Arial narrow, then you should place it in quotation marks like, font-family: "Arial narrow".
- The font-weight can be between 100 and 900.
- Normal=400 and bold=700

Example: 1.3
1. <!DOCTYPE HTML PUBLIC "-//W3C//DTD HTML 4.01//EN"
2. "http://www.w3.org/TR/html4/Strict.dtd">
3. <html>
4. <head>
5. <meta http-equiv="Content-Type" content="text/html; charset=iso-8859-1">
6. <title> CSS Simple Fonts</title>
7. <style type="text/css">
8. <!--
9. **H1** { font-family: san-serif; font-size: 14px;}
10. **H2** { font-size: 14pt; font-style: oblique;}
11. **H3**{ font-weight: bolder;}
12. -->
13. </style>
14. </head> <body>
15. <p>
16. <H1>San-serif, size 14px></H1>
17. <H2>Style oblique, size 14pt</H2>
18. <H3>Weight bolder</H3>
19. </p> </body>
20. </html>

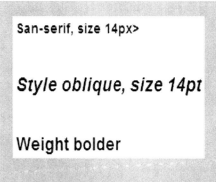

We used HTML tags H1, H2, H3 as selectors. Our H1 selector is **H1 { font-family: san-serif; font-size: 14px;}** when we call the H1 selector on line 16, it generates 14 pixels size and family of san-serif.

We can place them within only one selector like:
P {
font-family: san-serif;
font-size: 14px;
font-size: 14pt;
font-style: oblique;
font-weight: bolder;
}
As you see the code is simplified inside a bracket. The selector name "**P**" handles all of the properties and the related values. So anywhere inside the code, you can use the "P".

Example: 1.4
```
1.  <!DOCTYPE HTML PUBLIC "-//W3C//DTD HTML 4.01//EN"
2.  "http://www.w3.org/TR/html4/Strict.dtd">
3.  <html>
4.  <head>
5.  <meta http-equiv="Content-Type" content="text/html; charset=iso-8859-1">
6.  <title> CSS Simple Fonts</title>
7.  <style type="text/css">
<!--
8.  p{ font-family: san-serif; font-size: 14px;
9.  font-style: oblique;
10. font-weight: bolder;}
 -->
11. </style>
12. </head> <body>
13. <p>
14. This text is designed<br> according to the CSS
15. </p> </body>
16. </html>
```

This text is designed according to the CSS

Now you are familiar with the HTML selector. The HTML selector means using the HTML tags name as a *selector* name. As already mentioned, there is also the **CLASS** selector and the **ID** selector.
With either external or internal styles, the selector can be classified as:

Selectors: **HTML selector** (like P, I, B and so on)
Class selector
ID selector

Class selector

Previously we used the HTML selector with a preset style or inline style. Now we will use the **CLASS** selector. The class selector is good since you don't have to redefine the HTML selector entirely. In fact, you just use different styles within the source code. The general syntax for the CLASS selector:

.ClassSelector{property : value; }

Note: There is a *dot* in front of the selector.

Look at this example we use class selector to create two color boxes. We will use **XHTML *strict.dtd*** which forces us to check our code and compile it according to the strict regulation.

Example: 1.5

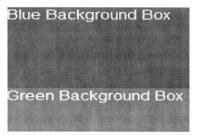

```
1.   <style type="text/css">
2.   .Box{
3.   width:170px;
4.   height:100px;
5.   }
6.   .Box1{background:blue; color:yellow}
7.   .Box2{background:green; color:white;}
8.   </style>

9.   <!DOCTYPE html PUBLIC "-//W3C//DTD XHTML 1.0 Strict//EN"
           "http://www.w3.org/TR/xhtml1/DTD/xhtml1-strict.dtd">
10.  <html xmlns="http://www.w3.org/1999/xhtml" lang="en">
11.  <head>
12.  <title>Font family </title>
13.  <meta http-equiv="Content-Type" content="text/html; charset=iso-8859-1" />
14.  </head> <body> <p>
15.  <div class="Box Box1">Blue Background Box</div>
16.  <div class="Box Box2"> Green Background Box </div>
17.  </div> </p> </body>
18.  </html>
```

First we declared CSS design with class Box (there is a dot front of box). The ".**Box** "is the top class which creates a box with 150 X 100px. We colored text and background with classes **Box1** and B**ox2** then on the line 15 and 16 we combined "Box Box1" and "Box Box2" therefore sizes are defined and colors also.

Older browser

Sometimes you may want to write a script that will run under modern and older browser therefore you use something like HTML comments. The CSS code will be closed inside the **<!- -** *and* **- ->**. Look at this example.

Example: 1.6

```
1. <!DOCTYPE HTML PUBLIC "-//W3C//DTD HTML 4.01//EN"
2. "http://www.w3.org/TR/html4/Strict.dtd">
3. <head>
4. <meta http-equiv="Content-Type" content="text/html; charset=iso-8859-1">
5. <title> Class Selector</title>
6. <style type="text/css">
     <!--
7. P.look {font-family: arial; font-size:16px; color :
   blue}
8. P.fonts { font-size: 20pt; color: maroon;}
9. hr{position: absolute; width:200px; left: 20px }
     -->
10. </style> </HEAD> <BODY>
11. <P class="look">The font 16px underline!
12. </P> <hr>
13. <P class="fonts">The font 20px Maroon! </P>
14. </BODY>
15. </HTML>
```

It recalls the classes that we are already called *look* and *fonts*. It produces different color text.

Note: We place the CSS code inside HTML comment. The above line **<!--** and **-->** is NOT a comment which compiler refuse to validate it, but we must use it. Why should we use it? The reality is that some old browsers do not validate the CSS code therefore they output the code itself as a text.

A class can be a dot like ".**words** "Then you can call it inside your code .Checkout this example.

Example: 1.7

```
1. <!DOCTYPE HTML PUBLIC "-//W3C//DTD HTML 4.01//EN"
2. "http://www.w3.org/TR/html4/Strict.dtd">
3. <head>
4. <meta http-equiv="Content-Type" content="text/html; charset=iso-8859-1">
5. <title> Class Selector</title>
6. <style type="text/css">
7. <!--
8. .Text{ font-size:14px;color:blue;}
9. -->
10. </STYLE>
11. </HEAD> <BODY>
12. <P> <SPAN CLASS= Text> Result of the
```

CLASS</SPAN>
13. Out of style!
14. <SPAN   STYLE="font-family: Arial;   font-size:10px; color: maroon;">
15. This is inline style</SPAN></P>
16. </BODY>
17. </HTML>

Result of the CLASS
Out of style!
This is inline style

Note: there is a dot at the front of Text on line 8.

ID Selector

Another way of using selector is by using ID selector. ID selector is used when you want to call a unique object with its related ID. It is usually used for different layers. The general syntax for ID selector:

#IDSelector { property : Value ; }

Example: 1.8
1. <!DOCTYPE HTML PUBLIC "-//W3C//DTD HTML 4.01//EN"
2. "http://www.w3.org/TR/html4/Strict.dtd">
3. <head>
4. <meta http-equiv="Content-Type" content="text/html; charset=iso-8859-1">
5. <title> ID Selector</title>
6. <style type="text/css">
7. #ID1 { background-color:yellow; width:25%; }
8. #ID2 { {font-family: arial; }
9. </style>
10. </head> <body>
11. <p id="ID1">Text background = yellow</p>
12. <p id="ID2">font-family=Arial</p>
13. </body> </html>

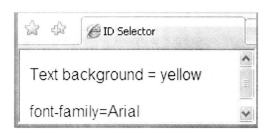

ID Selector

Text background = yellow

font-family=Arial

Group Class Selector

You can use grouped class styles which are several classes in one group. These classes are actually the same with only little differences. For example, there could be the same text and the same background color, but the fonts could be different.

.code1 *{font-family : "arial narrow"; color:red; background:blue; font-size:14pt;}*

.code2 *{font-family :"arial narrow"; color:red; background:blue; font-size:18pt;}*
You see that both classes are the same except that their fonts are different in size.
Now we know how to use styles in CSS. Therefore, the remaining CSS lessons will be extremely easy. We will start with formatting text and move on to more advanced features.

Example: 1.9
1. <!DOCTYPE HTML PUBLIC "-//W3C//DTD HTML 4.01//EN"
2. "http://www.w3.org/TR/html4/Strict.dtd">
3. <head>
4. <meta http-equiv="Content-Type" content="text/html; charset=iso-8859-1">
5. <title> CSS Fonts</title>
6. <style type="text/css">
7. <!--
8. span.font1 { font-family: san-serif; font-size: 14px;}
9. span.font2 { font-size: 14pt; font-style: oblique;}
10. span.font3 { font-weight: bolder;}
11. -->
12. </style>
13. </head> <body> <p>
14. <span class="font1">San-serif, size 14px> </span>
15. <span class="font2">Style oblique, size 14pt</span>
16. <span class="font3">Weight bolder</span>
17. </p> </body>
18. </html>

Span and div
We use span in the above example. By themselves, **div** and **span** do not cause any effect. They are, therefore, the best candidates for naming a CSS class. You will see many examples in CSS that use both span and div. The *div* and *span* do not style anything within the code, but we use them as HTML keywords.
Colors
We have already used CSS color in our code; here we bring more details about CSS colors. CSS provides the simplest way to create and manipulate colors. Color can be page background, text background and text color. You can use the color name like "**gray**", the color hexadecimal like "**#bebebe**" or the RGB(combination of Red, Green, Blue) like **rgb(190 190 190)**. All three forms produce the color gray. Unlike HTML, you do not need to create a table in order to use a specific text background with CSS.

Four ways to declare RGB:
- #rrggbb (e.g., #00FF00)
- #rgb (e.g., #0F0)
- rgb(int, int, int) where int is an integer between 0 and 255 like : rgb(10,232,00))
- rgb(X%,X%,X%) where X% is a percentage number between 0.0 and 100: rgb(0%,80%,0%)

Example: 1.10
```
1. <!DOCTYPE HTML PUBLIC "-//W3C//DTD HTML 4.01//EN"
2. "http://www.w3.org/TR/html4/Strict.dtd">
3. <head>
4. <meta http-equiv="Content-Type" content="text/html; charset=iso-8859-1">
5. <title> Different Backgrounds</title>
6. <style type="text/css">
7. <!--
8. body { background-color: yellow; }
9. div.textBack1 { background-color: gray; width:30%}
10. div.textBack2{ background-color: white; width:30%}
11. div.textColor{ background-color: white; color : #0000ff; width:30% }
12. -->
13. </style> </head> <body>
14. <h3>Yellow Page Background </h3>
15. <div class="textBack2"> <b> Background
    text is in white </b> </div>
16. <div class="textBack1"> <b> Background
    text is in gray! </b> </div>
17. <div class="textColor"><b> White
    background, blue text ! </b> </div>
18. </body>
19. </html>
```

To color text background:	div.textBack1 { background-color: gray; }
Text foreground:	div.textColor{ color: " #0000ff " }
You can use the RGB value:	div.textColor{ color:rgb(0 0 255) }
To color page background:	body { background-color: yellow; }

CSS background
The background can be a solid color set as the RGB, the color name, or the color hexadecimal value. We have already seen the background color in the previous example, **body { background-color: yellow; }**. Now we will work on the **background image**.

Background image
Background color provides many attributes such as Background-color, Background-image, Background-attachment, Background-repeat and Background-position.

Background names	Attributes
Background-image	url, none
Background-attachment	Fixed, scroll
Background-color	Repeat, repeat-x, repeat-y, no-repeat
Background-position	Percentage(%), pixel, top, bottom, left, right, center

You may attach the background image like this: **background-image:url ('phone.gif')**

Example: 1.11

```
1. <!DOCTYPE HTML PUBLIC "-//W3C//DTD HTML 4.01//EN"
2. "http://www.w3.org/TR/html4/Strict.dtd">
3. <head>
4. <meta http-equiv="Content-Type" content="text/html; charset=iso-8859-1">
5. <title> background images</title>
6. <style type="text/css">
7. <!--
8. body {
9. background-image:url('phone.gif') }
10. h3 {background-color:white; }
11. -->
12. </style>
13. </head>
14. <body>
15. <p> </p>
16. </body>
17. </html>
```

You may want to arrange your background so that lining up in a vertical format. Use **repeat-y;** in order to see the vertical background.
Check out this example.

Example: 1.12

```
1. <!DOCTYPE HTML PUBLIC "-//W3C//DTD HTML 4.01//EN"
2. "http://www.w3.org/TR/html4/Strict.dtd">
3. <head>
4. <meta http-equiv="Content-Type" content="text/html; charset=iso-8859-1">
5. <title> Vertical Images</title>
6. <style type="text/css">
7. <!--
8. body {
9. background-color: yellow;
10. background-image:url("c:\\pic1.jpg");
11. background-repeat: repeat-y; }
```

12. h3{text-align:center;}
13. -->
14. </style> </head>
15. <body>
16. <h3> Meidan Azadi
 Vertical Images </h3>
17. </body>
18. </html>

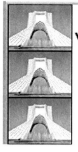

You can simply change **repeat-y** to **repeat-x** in the above example. You will then see the horizontal images.

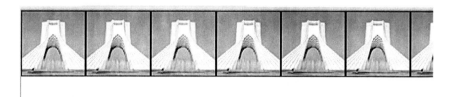

To load an image only once, use the **no-repeat** attribute.

    body
    {
    background-color: yellow;
    background-image:url('pic1.jpg');
    background-repeat: **no-repeat;**
    }

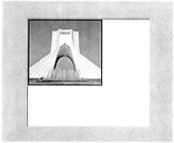

To see image in the center, add this line:
background-position: center;
An image can be placed on the left, right, top, bottom, center, and by percentage measures.

body
{
background-color: yellow;
background-image:url('pic1.jpg');
background-repeat: no-repeat;
background-position: 20% 80%;
}
It places an image 20% on the X-axis and 80% on the Y-axis.
You can use pixels like: 20px 60px

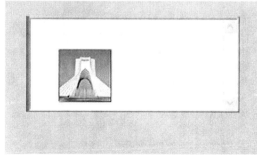

One interesting attribute is **fixed**. It does not let a loaded image scroll along with the text.

Example: 1.13
```
1. <!DOCTYPE HTML PUBLIC "-//W3C//DTD HTML 4.01//EN"
2. "http://www.w3.org/TR/html4/Strict.dtd">
3. <head>
4. <meta http-equiv="Content-Type" content="text/html; charset=iso-8859-1">
5. <title> Exact position</title>
6. <style type="text/css">
        <!--
7. body  {
8. background-color: yellow;
9. background-image:url('C:\\pic1.jpg');
10. background-repeat: no-repeat;
11. background-position: 10% 10%;
12. background-attachment : fixed;
13. }
        -->
14. </style> </head>
15. <body>
16. <h2>********************
17. *************************
18. *************************
19. *************************
20. *************************</h2>
21. </body>
22. </html>
```

Try to **minimize** the browser to see the active scroll. Then up and down scrollbar to see only text will move without effecting the image. Now use this code to bring the picture to the center and to stop it from being scrollable:

Body
{
background:url('pic1.jpg')
no-repeat fixed center;
}

Resize background

The background can be resized according to width and height. This can be done by the amount of pixels or percentages. You can also use **border** thickness and other border attributes which we will discuss later on.
```
div.background  {
 width: 300px;
 height: 200px;
 background: url(c:\\pic1.jpg) repeat;
 border: 2px solid black;   }
```

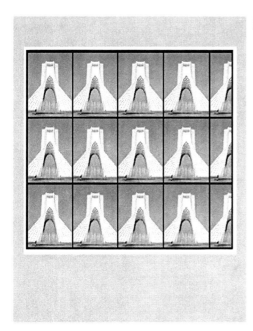

Example: 1.14

1. <!DOCTYPE HTML PUBLIC "-//W3C// DTD HTML 4.01//EN"
2. "http://www.w3.org/TR/html4/Strict.dtd">
3. <head>
4. <meta   http-equiv="Content-Type"   content ="text/html; charset=iso-8859-1">
5. <title> height, width</title>
6. <style type="text/css">
7. <!--
8. div.background {
9. width: 300px; height: 200px;
10. background: url(c:\\pic1.jpg) repeat;
11. border: 2px solid black; }
12. -->
13. </style> </head> <body>
14.   <div class="background"></div>
15. </body>
16. </html>

If the image is not loaded then the border will be shown on the screen. The border can be solid black, as you can see in the example.

CSS comments

Comments are design to describe the code. This feature does not have any effect on the browser. In fact, the browser never reads it. The comment is like this, */* comment */*
For example:

```
div.background  /*class background*/
{
width: 300px; /*width 300 pixel this just comment*/
height: 200px;
background: url(c:\\pic1.jpg) repeat;
```

Review questions

1- Why CSS
2- What is the selector?
3- Write the general syntax for CSS selector.
4- Write a statement to display an image as the background.
5- Write a statement to control the image position.
6- Give an example of font size and style.
7- Write a statement to control the image (NOT MOVE WITH TEXT).
8- Fix this statement **dlv.textColor{ colors : grb(10 10 255) }**
9- What is inline style in CSS?
10- How do you set a background width and height?

Answers

1- To develop web page and help HTML code.
2- The selector is essential to the CSS code; we declare it and then use it in the body of the code.
3- Selector{property: value;}
4- Background :url(path)
5- **background-position: center;**
6- Font-size: 14pt; font-style:normal;
7- background-attachment: fixed;
8- **div.textColor{ color : rgb(10 10 255) }**
9- You directly change color, fonts and so on, anywhere inside your code.
10- div.background

```
{
width: 300px;
height: 200px;
background: url(c:\\pic1.jpg) repeat;
border: 2px solid black;
}
```

Chapter 2

Formatting Text in CSS

- Introduction
- CSS border
- Text properties
- Margin
- Padding
- CSS lists

- Different list shapes
- CSS table
- Simple table
- Alternative colors
- Managing table
- Laboratory exercises

Introduction

CSS provides great formatting features for text. You can simply set your style within the head part and use your per-styles within the HTML code. It is interesting to know that with CSS you can create tables that look like image graphics. Through the manipulation of the border, color, padding and so on, the borders and cells of object can be really attractive. You can easily change the margin, space and height of the font to your desired format. In this chapter we try to bring the most attractive features of CSS.

We must continue the topics from the last chapter. Here we look at the CSS border.

CSS border

CSS is enriched in border attributes used to manipulate the border. In many cases, the combination of different border attributes makes a difference. The webpage must use a border that is related to the content of the page.

Properties	Values	Example
border-bottom-width border-left-width border-width border-top-width border-right-width	thin, medium, thick, length	border-bottom-width: thin
border-top-color border-right-color border-bottom-color border-left-color border-color	Any color, Use RGB, color name or hexadecimal value	border-right-color: blue or border-bottom-color: #CCCCCC

border-bottom-style border-left-style border-style border-top-style border-right-style	none, solid, double, groove, ridge, inset, outset You can use a combination of several attributes.	border-right-style: groove border-style: dotted border-style: hidden border-style: solid
border-top border-right border-bottom border-left border	*border-width ,border-style , border-color*	border-bottom: thick inset yellow

This example shows the different types of border design. You can design various borders with CSS border attributes.

Example: 2.1

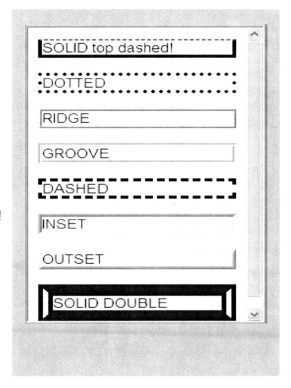

1.   <!DOCTYPE HTML PUBLIC "-//W3C//DTD HTML 4.01//EN"
2.   "http://www.w3.org/TR/html4/Strict.dtd">
3.   <head>
4.   <meta http-equiv="Content-Type" content="text/html; charset=iso-8859-1">
5.   <title> CSS Borders</title>
6.   <style type="text/css">
7.   <!--
8.   p.solid {border-style: solid; border-top: thin blue dashed;}
9.   p.dot {border-style: dotted}
10. p.rid {border-style: ridge; }
11. p.grv {border-style: groove }
12. p.dash {border-style: dashed; }
13. p.inset {border-style: inset; }
14. p.outset {border-style: outset; }
15. p.sdouble {border-style: solid double;border-width:15px}
16. -->
17. </style> </head> <body>
18. <p class="solid"> SOLID top dashed! </p>
19. <p class="dot">DOTTED</p>
20. <p class="rid">RIDGE</p>
21. <p class="grv">GROOVE</p>
22. <p class="dash">DASHED</p>
23. <p class="inset">INSET</p>
24. <p class="outset">OUTSET</p>
25. <p class="sdouble">SOLID DOUBLE</p>
26. </body> </html>

Various combinations of colors, styles and size can make an appealing image on the screen. Here we will try to put them together in order to create a nice frame.

Example: 2.2
```
1.  <!DOCTYPE HTML PUBLIC "-//W3C//DTD HTML 4.01//EN"
2.  "http://www.w3.org/TR/html4/Strict.dtd">
3.  <head>
4.  <meta http-equiv="Content-Type" content="text/html; charset=iso-8859-1">
5.  <title> Fancy Border</title>
6.  <style type="text/css">
        <!--
7.  div {
8.  border-left-style: ridge;
9.  border-left-color: maroon;
10. border-left-width: 30px;
11. border-bottom-style: ridge;
12. border-bottom-color: yellow;
13. border-bottom-width: 30px;
14. border-right-style: ridge;
15. border-right-color: maroon;
16. border-right-width: 30px;
17. border-top-style: ridge;
18. border-top-color: yellow;
19. border-top-width: 30px;
20. }
        -->
21. </style></head> <body>
22. <h2>CSS Borders</h2>
23. <div><b>Nice border on screen!</b></div>
24. </body>
25. </html>
```

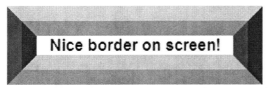

As you see the above frame is most look like to a 3D image. In fact this is just one of beauty of CSS. You can use such concept to design the webpage layout.

Text properties

There are many text properties that help us to design text inside the webpage. We will cover most of them in some easy to understand examples.
Look at some of the basic text properties.

Properties	Value	Example
letter-spacing	Normal, *length*	letter-spacing:4pt
vertical-align	Sub, super	vertical-align:sub
text-decoration	none, underline, overline, line-through	text-decoration:none
text-transform	capitalize, uppercase, lowercase, none	text-transform: lowercase
text-align	left, right, center, justify	text-align: center
text-indent	*Length, percentage*	text-indent:10px
line-height	normal, *number, length, percentage*	line-height:normal
white-space	normal, pre, nowrap	White-space:normal

Letter-spacing causes some spaces between characters. You can use pixels to manage these spaces. Text-transform can change whole texts to "capitalize format", in which every letter of the first word will be capitalized.

Example: 2.3

```
1.  <!DOCTYPE HTML PUBLIC "-//W3C//DTD HTML 4.01//EN"
2.  "http://www.w3.org/TR/html4/Strict.dtd">
3.  <head>
4.  <meta http-equiv="Content-Type" content="text/html; charset=iso-8859-1">
5.  <title> Formatting Text</title>
6.  <style type="text/css">
7.  <!--
8.  div.space1 {letter-spacing: 1px}  div.space2{letter-spacing: 0.2cm}
9.  div.transform{text-transform:capitalize}
10. div.height{line-height:300%}
11. -->
12. </style> </head> <body> <div>
13. <div class="space1">Character spaces at 5px</div>
14. <div class="space2">Character spaces at 0.2cm </div>
15. <div class="transform">text is capitalized</div>
16. <div class="height">Line height is 300</div>
17. </div> </body> </html>
```

```
Character spaces at 5px
C h a r a c t e r   s p a c e s   a t   0 . 2 c m
T e x t   I s   C a p i t a l i z e d

L i n e   H e i g h t   I s   3 0 0
```

Margin

Margin helps to place a text onto the page. It provides four attribute sides: right, left, bottom and top. Each side can be measured by px or pt.

Margin Properties		
Properties	**Value**	**Example**
margin-top	*length*, *percentage*, auto	margin-top:5px
margin-bottom		margin-bottom:5em
margin-left		margin-left:5pt
margin-right		margin-right:5px
margin		margin:15px 5px 10px 15px

If you want to use four values, you can use four values like {margin: 5px 5px 5px 5px} more simply than top, bottom, left and right.

- First value = top
- Second value = right
- Third value = bottom
- Forth value = left

If you only use two values, they will be the top and bottom:
{margin: 5px 5px } This means Top=5px bottom=5px

Example: 2.4
```
1.    <!DOCTYPE HTML PUBLIC "-//W3C//DTD HTML 4.01//EN"
2.    "http://www.w3.org/TR/html4/Strict.dtd">
3.    <head>
4.    <meta http-equiv="Content-Type" content="text/html; charset=iso-8859-1">
5.    <title> Text Margin</title>
6.    <style type="text/css">
7.    <!--
8.    <style type="text/css">
9.    div.Margin1{margin-right: 20px;
10.   margin-top:5px;
11.   margin-bottom: 10px;  margin-left: 0px;
12.   border: thin black dashed; }
```

13. div.Margin2{margin-right: 20px;
14. margin-top:20px; margin-bottom: 0px;
15. margin-left: 100px; border: 5px dashed; }
16. div.Margin3{margin:10px 10px 10px 10px ;
17. border: 5px solid red; }
18. -->
19. </style> </head> <body>
20. <div>
21. <div class="Margin1">The text left margin is: 0 </div>
22. <div class="Margin2">The text left margin is:100</div>
23. <div class="Margin3">The text left margin is:10</div>
24. </div> </body> </html>

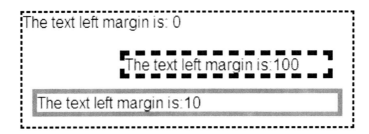

Note: We use border along with margin to show the margin on the screen. In fact, just look at the border to see how far away it is placed from the main border.

Padding

CSS padding is like the CSS margin except that there is white space between margins or between actual contents.

padding-top, padding-right, padding-bottom, and padding-left.
For example:
p { padding: 5px 5px 5px 5px; }
The **BOX MODLING** has five properties:

- height
- width
- margin
- border
- padding

Padding Properties		
Property	**Value**	**Example**
padding-top	*length, percentage*	**padding-top:12%**
padding-bottom		**padding-bottom: 2em**
padding-right		**padding-right:15px**
padding-left		**padding-left:15pt; }**
padding	Four value	**padding: 10px 5px 12px 15px**

Example: 2.5
1. <!DOCTYPE HTML PUBLIC "-//W3C//DTD HTML 4.01//EN"
2. "http://www.w3.org/TR/html4/Strict.dtd">
3. <head>
4. <meta http-equiv="Content-Type" content="text/html; charset=iso-8859-1">
5. <title> Padding</title>
6. <style type="text/css">
7. <!--
8. div.border{border:5px dashed; width:50%} /*5px from every edges*/
9. div.padd {
10. background-color:yellow;
11. padding:10px; /*size of padding*/
12. margin:20px; }   /*Margin 20px from border*/
13. -->
14. </style> </head> <body>
15. <div class="border">
16. <div class="padd">Padding is set to 10px, Border, Margin, Padding.</div>
17. </div> </body>
18. </html>

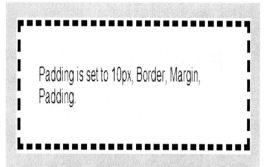

You can see that the border is in a dashed line. You can also see a margin between the border and the padding. The last one is in yellow, indicating an area of padding.

On line 9 you will see **margin: 20px**, meaning that the margin is set to be 10 pixels in all directions (*top=20px, bottom=20px, right=20px, left=20px*).

CSS lists

A CSS list provides a wide variety of options. In addition to the many attributes, you can attach your own bullet to the list. Look at some properties that are listed here.

List Properties

Property	Value	Example
list-style-position	inside outside	**ol { list-style-position:inside; } ul { list-style-position:outside; }**
list-style-image	URL	**ul { list-style-image:url(image1.jpg); }**
list-style	Can declare multiple attributes list-style-type list-style-position list-style-image	**ul { list-style:disc inside url(image.gif); }**
marker-offset	auto	**ol:before { display:marker; marker-offset:3px; }**

list-style-type	disc, circle, square decimal decimal-leading-zero lower-roman upper-roman lower-alpha upper-alpha lower-greek lower-latin upper-latin hebrew armenian georgian cjk-ideographic hiragana katakana hiragana-iroha katakana-iroha	ol { list-style-type: lower-latin; } ul { list-style-type:circle; }

Different list shapes

In this example you will see a circle shape, square shape, disc shape and a bullet shape. The bullet is attached by reading from the image file. The **bul1.gif** is the image file that exists in the folder and we can simply call it.

Example: 2.6

1. <!DOCTYPE HTML PUBLIC "-//W3C//DTD HTML 4.01//EN"
2. "http://www.w3.org/TR/html4/Strict.dtd">
3. <head>
4. <meta http-equiv="Content-Type" content="text/html; charset=iso-8859-1">
5. <title> CSS List</title>
6. <style type="text/css">
7. <!--
8. ul.disc {list-style-type: disc}
9. ul.circle {list-style-type: circle}
10. ul.square {list-style-type: square}
11. ul.image{ list-style-image:url(c:\\bul1.gif);}
12. -->
13. </style> </head> <body>
14. <ul class="disc"><li> Bananas</li></ul>
15. <ul class="circle"><li> Grapes </li></ul>
16. <ul class="square"><li> Apples </li></ul>
17. <ul class="image"><li> Oranges </li></ul>
18. </body> </html>

You can use such features as background, margin and padding along with the list. In this example we use a table in order to show the different list attributes.

Example: 2.7

1. <!DOCTYPE HTML PUBLIC "-//W3C// DTD HTML 4.01//EN"
2. "http://www.w3.org/ TR/html4/Strict.dtd">
3. <head>
4. <meta http-equiv= "Content-Type" content ="text/html; charset=iso-8859-1">
5. <title> Different List Styles</title>
6. <style type="text/css">
7. <!--
8. ul.disc {list-style-type: disc}
9. ol.list1 {
10. list-style-type: circle; }
11. ol.list2 { list-style-type: square; }
12. ol.list3 { list-style-type: upper-roman;}
13. ol.list4 {list-style-image: url(arrow.gif);}
14. -->
15. </style> </head>
16. <body>
17. <table border=1>
18. <tr> <td>
19. <ol class="list1">
20. <li> Red</li> <li> Blue </li>
21. <li> Yellow</li> </ol> </td>
22. <td><ol class="list2">
23. <li> Red</li> <li> Blue </li> <li> Yellow</li></ol></td>
24. <td><ol class="list3">
25. <li> Red</li> <li> Blue </li> <li> Yellow</li></ol></td>
26. <td><ol class="list4">
27. <li> Red</li> <li> Blue </li> <li> Yellow</li></ol></td>
28. </tr> </table>
29. </body> </html>

▶The arrow in the out is obtained from a file. The image file is called **arrow.gif**. You can download any thumbnail image and use it within the list.

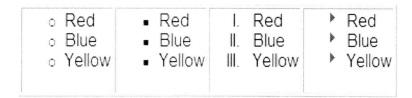

CSS tables

A table is a way of displaying data. When you want to display data on screen, you need some form of tabular format. Many programmers make different designs and layouts for their tables. CSS provides sufficient properties to format a table according to data needs. Use the <table>, <TR>,<TD> and <TH>tags to build your table.

Use the <caption> tag to create caption for the table.

<caption> *This is a simple table*</caption>

Use the <TH> tag to format your header:

TH { text-align: center; font-weight: bold }

Table Properties in CSS

Property	Value
border-collapse	collapse separate
border-spacing	length length
caption-side	top bottom left right
empty-cell	show hide
table-layout	auto fixed

Simple table

The table-layout determines how a table should be laid out. It can be automatic or fixed. If you use a fixed cell then it does not stretch along with the data size.
table-layout: automatic
table-layout: fixed
You can set the height and width of the cell.

Example: 2.8

```
1.  <!DOCTYPE HTML PUBLIC "-//W3C//DTD HTML 4.01//EN"
2.  "http://www.w3.org/TR/html4/Strict.dtd">
3.  <head>
4.  <meta http-equiv="Content-Type" content="text/html; charset=iso-8859-1">
5.  <title> Basic Table in CSS</title>
6.  <style type="text/css">
7.  <!--
8.  table.format1 {
9.  table-layout: automatic
10. }
11. table.format2 {table-layout:fixed  }
12. -->
13. </style></head><body>
14. <table class="format1" border="1" width="100%">
15. <caption> This is an automatic table</caption>
16. <tr> <td>This automatic cell handles a large size of data</td>
17. <td width="70%">This automatic cell handles a large size of data</td>
18. </tr> </table>
19. <table class="format2" border="1" width="100%">
20. <caption>This is a fixed cell</caption>
21. <tr><td>This automatic cell handles a large size of data</td>
22. <td>This automatic cell handles a large size of data</td>
23. </tr></table></body> </html>
```

This is an automatic table

This automatic cell handles a large size of data	This automatic cell handles a large size of data

This is a fixed cell

This automatic cell handles a large size of data	This automatic cell handles a large size of data

Alternative colors

We can color each cell alternatively with CSS. For example, we can have the first row in yellow and the second row in white. The third row will automatically will be in yellow again and the pattern will continue.

Example: 2.9

```
1.  <!DOCTYPE HTML PUBLIC "-//W3C//DTD HTML 4.01//EN"
2.  "http://www.w3.org/TR/html4/Strict.dtd">
3.  <head>
4.  <meta http-equiv="Content-Type" content="text/html; charset=iso-8859-1">
5.  <title> Alternative color</title>
6.  <style type="text/css">
7.  <!--
8.  tr.ALT1 td {
9.  background-color: #FC0; color: black; }
10. tr.ALT2 td {
11. background-color: #99FFCC; color: rgb(0,0,0); }
12. -->
13. </style></head>
14. <body><table>
15. <tr class="ALT1"> <td>Rent </td>
    <td>$679</td></tr>
16. <tr class="ALT2"><td>Telephone </td>
    <td>$46.95</td> </tr>
17. <tr class="ALT1"> <td>Hydro</td> <td>$125.55
    </td> </tr>
18. <tr class="ALT2"> <td>Internet </td>
    <td>$46.25</td></tr>
19. </table> </body>
20. </html>
```

Rent	$679
Telephone	$46.95
Hydro	$125.55
Internrt	$46.25

Managing table

A CSS table can have a better look and display data in an effective way.

Example: 2.10

```
1.  <!DOCTYPE HTML PUBLIC "-//W3C//DTD HTML 4.01//EN"
2.  "http://www.w3.org/TR/html4/Strict.dtd">
```

3.   <head>
4.   <meta http-equiv="Content-Type" content="text/html; charset=iso-8859-1">
5.   <title> Design Nice Table</title>
6.   <style type="text/css">
7.   <!--
8.   table {background: blue; border: 10px ridge yellow; margin: 10px; }
9.   TD {
10. background: white; border: outset 5pt; vertical-align: right;
11. padding: 14px; }
12. CAPTION {
13. border-left-style: ridge; border-left-color: yellow; border-left-width: 10px;
14. border-bottom-style: ridge;
15. border-bottom-color: yellow;
16. border-bottom-width: 10px;
17. border-right-style: ridge;
18. border-right-color: yellow;
19. border-right-width: 10px;
20. border-top-style: ridge;
21. border-top-color: yellow;
22. border-top-width: 10px;
23. }
24. -->
25. </style></head>
26. <body>
27. <table>
28. <caption>Students Expenses Amount</caption>
29. <tfoot><tr>
30. <td colspan="2">Total Amounts: 4851.50</td>
31. </tr></tfoot>
32. <tbody><tr>
33. <td>Fall Expenses</td>
34. <td>$1500.00</td>
35. </tr><tr>
36. <td>Winter Expenses</td>
37. <td>$1700.55.00</td>
38. </tr><tr>
39. <td>Spring Expenses</td>
40. <td>$1650.95</td>
41. </tr></tbody>
42. </table></body></HTML>

Students Expenses Amount	
Fall Expenses	$1500.00
Winter Expenses	$1700.55.00
Spring Expenses	$1650.95
Total Amounts: 4851.50	

The CAPTION, which starts from line 14 and continues to line 31, is written to create a nice caption with a ridge of yellow color. This frame has already been seen in this chapter. Change <tfoot></tfoot> to <thead></thead> on line 32 and observe the result.

Students Expenses Amount	
Total Amounts: 4851.50	
Fall Expenses	$1500.00
Winter Expenses	$1700.55.00
Spring Expenses	$1650.95

Laboratory exercises

1-With the power of CSS, create a layout that divides a page into three portions.

    1- Top Header (20% width): Set the company logo
    2- Left (20%): Place for the site navigation
    3- Right (80%): The main site.

2- Create the table and design it with CSS attributes. The design depends on your artistic abilities. The table must be floatable. This means that it enlarges as the caption gets bigger.

Chapter 3

Link and Image Effects

- Introduction
- CSS Link
- CSS text decoration
- Mouse activation
- Link decoration
- Cursor manipulation
- Overflow
- Creating external CCS
- Linking external CSS file

- CSS Multi-page headers
- Positioning Images
- Shadow position effect
- Alpha effect
- Blur effect
- FlipH & FlipV
- Wave effect
- More effects
- Laboratory exercises

Introduction

Perhaps the linkage is one of the important parts of webpage design. CSS Cascading Style Sheets has magnificent features that allow us to work with the link and implement the images. In this chapter we will learn about all the important aspects of CSS and we will demonstrate interesting mouse shapes and mouse behavior. We will demonstrate how to work with images

CSS Link

Link in CSS facilitates the page linkage. There are four selectors:

- A:link
- A:visited
- A:active
- A:hover

A:link is used for a new link.
A:visited is used for a visited link.
A:active is used for an activate the link when you click on it.
A:hover is used for when the mouse hovers over the link (e.g. changes color).

Example: 3.1

```
1.    <!DOCTYPE HTML PUBLIC "-//W3C//DTD HTML 4.01//EN"
2.    "http://www.w3.org/TR/html4/Strict.dtd">
3.    <head>
4.    <meta http-equiv-"Content-Type" content="text/html; charset=iso-8859-1">
5.    <title> Link</title>
6.    <style type="text/css">
```

7. <!--
8. body{background-color: yellow;}
9. -->
10. </style> </head> <body>
11. <p> <a href="http://www.yahoo.com"> Visit Yahoo Site</a>
12. </p> </body> </html>

Visit Yahoo Site

This is a simple link. If you click on this link, it goes to the yahoo site. Now, there is a little problem on the above link: You can see that there is a little unwanted bar under the "*Visit Yahoo Site*". To get rid of this bar you need the CSS **text-decoration** selector.

CSS text decoration

Usually we use text decoration along with the CSS link. If the "*text-decoration: none*" attribute is set, then there will not be any bar under the link.

CSS Text-Decoration Properties		
Properties	**Values**	**Example**
text-decoration	*none* *underline* *overline* *line-through* *blink (not supported in IE>*	text-decoration:none text-decoration:underline text-decoration:overline text-decoration:line-through text-decoration:blink

text-decoration:none means that there will not be any decoration around the selected text
text-decoration:underline returns an underline bar
text-decoration:overline returns an over line bar
text-decoration:line-through returns a bar through the text
text-decoration:blink returns blinking but does not work under **IE**

Mouse activation

In this example, simply place the mouse over the link and do not click. You will see it change from **overline** to **underline** and the background will become yellow.

Place mouse over link, don't click!

See Yahoo Engin

Example: 3.2
1. <!DOCTYPE HTML PUBLIC "-//W3C//DTD HTML 4.01//EN"
2. "http://www.w3.org/TR/html4/Strict.dtd">
3. <head>
4. <meta http-equiv="Content-Type" content= "text/html; charset=iso-8859-1">
5. <title> Link Decoration</title>

By placing the mouse on the link, the bar moves on the top of the link and the background becomes yellow.

Place mouse over link, don't click!

See Yahoo Engin

6. `<style type="text/css">`
7. `<!--`
8. `<head> <style type="text/css">`
9. `.decore A:link {text-decoration: none}`
10. `.decore A:visited {text-decoration: none}`
11. `.decore A:active {text-decoration: overline}`
12. `.decore A:hover {text-decoration: underline;`
        `background-color:yellow; color: balck;}`
13. `-->`
14. `</style> </head> <body>`
15. `<h3> Place mouse over link, don't click! </h3>`
16. `<div class="decore">`
17. `<a href="http://www.yahoo.com">See Yahoo Engine`
        `</a>`
18. `</div> </body>`
19. `</html>`

Link decoration

Here you can see another example where mouse-over causes bigger font, overline, underline and background color effects.

```
decore A:link {text-decoration: none}
.decore A:visited {text-decoration:none; color:black; font-size:15pt}
.decore A:active {text-decoration: none}
.decore A:hover {text-decoration: underline overline;
background-color:yellow; color: maroon;font-size:25pt}
```

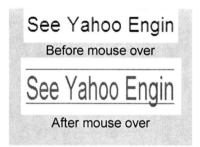

See Yahoo Engin
Before mouse over

See Yahoo Engin
After mouse over

Cursor manipulation

The shape of the cursor can have different indications. For example, when the cursor looks like this shape ⌛ , we understand that we have to wait. When the shape becomes like this shape ▷? , we know that this means help. To use the relevant cursor shape, use this style: **Shape1 {cursor:help}** (this produces the help shape). We put the most important shapes in action in this example.

Shape	Name	Shape	Name	Shape	Name
▷	**default**	▷?	**help**	⇐	**w-resize**
+	**crosshair**	⇧	**n-resize**	▷	**nw-resize**

	hand		ne-resize		progress
	pointer		e-resize		not-allowed
	move		se-resize		no-drop
	text		s-resize		vertical-text
	wait		sw-resize		all-scroll
	col-resize		row-resize		url

Example: 3.3

```
1.   <!DOCTYPE HTML PUBLIC "-//W3C//DTD HTML 4.01//EN"
2.   "http://www.w3.org/TR/html4/Strict.dtd">
3.   <head>
4.   <meta http-equiv="Content-Type" content="text/html; charset=iso-8859-1">
5.   <title> Cursor Shapes</title>
6.   <style type="text/css">
7.   <!--
8.   A{text-decoration:none}
9.   .hand {cursor:HAND;}
10.  .help{cursor:HELP;}
11.  .move{cursor:MOVE;}
12.  .wait{cursor:WAIT;}
13.  .all{cursor:all-scroll;}
14.  .not{cursor:not-allowed;}
        -->
15.  </style></head><body> <p><b>
16.  <a href="" class="hand"> HAND</a><br>
17.  <a href="" class="help"> HELP </a><br>
18.  <a href="" class= "move"> MOVE</a><br>
19.  <a href="" class="wait">WAIT</a><br>
20.  <a href="" class="all">ALL-SCROLL </a> <br>
21.  <a href="" class="not">NOT-ALLOWED </a>
22.  </b></p>
23.  </body> </html>
```

```
HAND
HELP
MOVE
WAIT
ALL-SCROLL
NOT-ALLOWED
```

The above example produces cursor shapes. Just place your mouse on the link to see the shape of the cursor.

Overflow

Sometimes you need to use overflow text in order to occupy less spaces. The overflow property is as follows:

Overflow properties	
Visible	Default
Hidden	Does not display scrollbar
Auto	Automatic display of scroll when text is large
Scroll	Display scrollbar

Example: 3.4

1. <!DOCTYPE HTML PUBLIC "-//W3C//DTD HTML 4.01//EN"
2. "http://www.w3.org/TR/html4/Strict.dtd">
3. <head>
4. <meta http-equiv="Content-Type" content="text/html; charset=iso-8859-1">
5. <title> Text overflow</title>
6. <style type="text/css">
7. <!--
8. .overflow {
9. background-color:yellow;
10. text-align:justify; width:140px;
11. height:120px; overflow: scroll }
12. -->
13. </style></head><body>
14. <H5>The overflow scrollbar!</H5>
15. <div class="overflow">
16. We can control the large text to overflow into a little box. It does not occupy a large space!
17. </div></body></html>

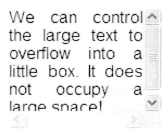

On line 7, the **text-align:justify;** is used justify the text to the right and the left equally. If you set the **overflow:scroll** to **overflow:hidden** on line 10, then you will see that this image has no scrollbar.

we can control the
large text to be
overlown in a little
box. It dose not
occupy some large
space!

Creating external CCS

Up until now we have worked with internal styles, or the inline style. Now we must see how the external style works. Why do we need to create an external file in CSS? Well, sometimes we need to create a styled file and use it in several pages. For example, if you want your logo, along with the desired colors and fonts, to be repeatedly displayed on the top of each page, you only need to create it once. You simply call it whenever you want it to reappear. Creating a CSS style sheet file is easy. Open your Notepad or any text editor, type your code in CSS format and save the file as **anyName.css**. Remember that the file must be saved with a **css** extension (lowercase) and NOT with an html extension. Since your file must be saved with a css extension, you do not need to include the **<style type="text/css">** tag.

Linking external CSS file

To link the external style sheet you just put the linkage code inside the page. Where the code should be placed? It should be placed between the <head> and the </head> tags. You could create a style sheet file, call it **design.css,** and then put this code inside the head tag of each page.
<HEAD>
<link rel="stylesheet" type="text/css" href="design.css">
</HEAD>

Steps to create CSS files

1- Open your text-editor (*Notepad*) and type this code:

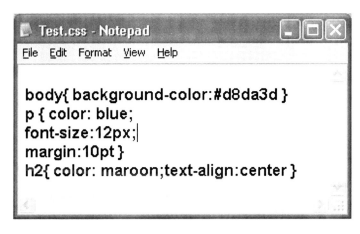

```
Test.css - Notepad
File  Edit  Format  View  Help

body{ background-color:#d8da3d }
p { color: blue;
font-size:12px;
margin:10pt }
h2{ color: maroon;text-align:center }
```

2- Save it as **Test.css** and close this file.
3- Again, open another blank Notepad and type this code:

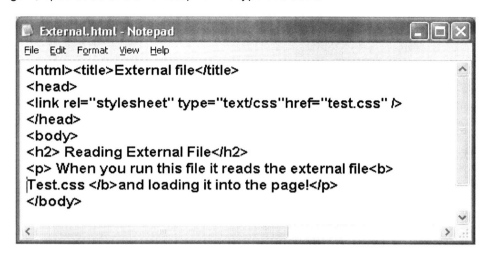

4- Save it as **External.html** then try to run this file (under Windows Explorer, double click on External.html>)

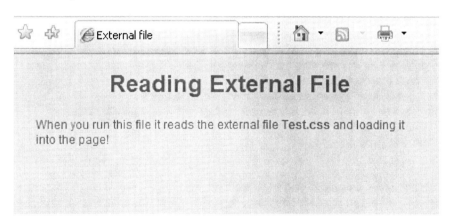

Using the external file can be very beneficial. First, if you want to change something in the design, you do not need to change the code for every single page. Once a change is made in the file, Test.css, it will automatically affect all the pages that call this file. The code also becomes very small and runs faster.

The **<LINK>** tag inside the head, assigned to media type-text/css, is a linking document. If the browser does not support it then the browser ignores it. The LINK tag takes **media** option as follows:
<LINK REL=StyleSheet HREF="myfile.css" TYPE="text/css"
 Style" **MEDIA**="screen">

- **Screen**: default value
- **Print**: for printer
- **Aural**: for speech
- **Braille**: for Braille
- **Tv**: for television
- **All**: for all output devices

You can use multi-declarations such as,
<LINK REL=StyleSheet HREF="myfile.css" TYPE="text/css"
Style" MEDIA="screen, print">

The REL specifies the CSS file in the HTML file. It can be used as **alternative**.
<LINK REL=Alternate StyleSheet HREF="Test.css" TYPE="text/css"
Style" MEDIA="screen, print">

Alternate means that if the preferred file is not loaded in the page then it uses the alternative file.

CSS Multi-page headers

Sometimes you might need one header for all the pages. You might also create a nice header for all the pages but want the topics inside the header to be different. Once you create the styles, you can use them many times. In this example we will create a header for all of the html pages and we will call that header to be displayed on the top of each page. It is so easy to have several files and it is a good way to always save your program code into different files. First you just save your CSS design as a file with **.css** extension like (myfile.css) then call this file in your html file.

<link rel="stylesheet" type="text/css"href="mufile.css">

Watch this file. I save this file as **style.css** in fact it is just one line code.

```
<!--
body{color:red; font-size:40px;}
-->
```

The *comment* part is an option you can use it or not.
Then I call the **style.css** into my html file. Here is my html file that I save it as **Seelt.html**.

```
<!DOCTYPE HTML PUBLIC "-//W3C//DTD HTML 4.01//EN"
"http://www.w3.org/TR/html4/Strict.dtd">
 <head>
 <meta http-equiv="Content-Type" content="text/html; charset=iso-8859-1">
<title>Image Border Effect</title>
<link rel="stylesheet" type="text/css"href="d1.css">
 </style>  </head> <body>
<p> Welcome </p>
</body>
</HTML>
```

After run the **SeeIt.html**, it produces this result with font=40px and color- red.

Welcome

Here you have three files. All files must be saved in the same directory; you need to give the exact path if you save it in a different directory.

#1 Save this decoration file as: **header.css**

body {background:#FFCC00;}
div {
background: #d8da3d;   border: outset 5pt;
padding: 14px;
font-family:forte, arial;   font-size:20pt;
font-weight:bold;   text-align: center;
border-left-style: ridge;   border-left-color: yellow;
border-left-width: 10px; border-bottom-style: ridge;
border-bottom-color: yellow; border-bottom-width: 10px;
border-right-style: ridge; border-right-color: yellow;
border-right-width: 10px; border-top-style: ridge;
border-top-color: yellow; border-top-width: 10px;
}

#2 save this file as: **Page1.html**

```
1.  <!DOCTYPE HTML PUBLIC "-//W3C//DTD HTML 4.01//EN"
2.  "http://www.w3.org/TR/html4/Strict.dtd">
3.  <head>
4.  <meta http-equiv="Content-Type" content="text/html; charset=iso-8859-1">
5.  <title> CSS Design</title>
6.  <link rel="stylesheet" type="text/css"href="header.css">
7.  </style>
8.  </head>
9.  <body>
10. <div>Welcome to CSS Technologia</div>
11. <H3>Introduction to CSS</h3>
12. <p>
13. <a href="page2.html"> See Next Page</a>
14. </p>
15. </body>
16. </html>
```

#3 Save this file as: **Page2.html**
| ```html
<html><title>External file Page2</title>
<head>
<link rel="stylesheet" type="text/css"href="header.css" />
</head>
<body>
Advanced Topics In CSS
<H3> Advanced CSS Chapter </h3>
<a href="page1.html"> Back to Page1 </a>
</body>
</html>
``` |

Click on the link "**See Next Page**". You will see the same frame header but it will have different text.

Try to add *absolute positions* to your decoration file (**header.css**), and then run your file.

```
position: absolute;
width:80%;
margin-top:1em;
```
```

margin-left:10%;

▍▶ Note: For simplicity we put CSS and HTML into the same file, but you can put them into several different files.

Positioning Images

There are many great ways to manipulate images, text and other aspects of a web page with CSS. Resizing an image is possible by using **height** and **width**. The position of an image can be relative or absolute. Filter is a very interesting feature of CSS. The filter lets us play around with the image without having to use any particular graphics software.

▍▶ Note: Filter works on the text that height and width has defined.

Filter name	Effect
Filter: alpha	Creates opacity that becomes light by the end
Filter: blur	Creates blurred object
Filter: chroma	Works with image, makes image transparent
Filter: dropshadow	Creates dropping shadow along X and y with specified color
Filter: glow	Creates some glow around the object
Filter: shadow	Something between dropshadow and glow
Filter: flipH	Flipping horizontally
Filter: flipV	Flipping vertically
Filter: grayscale	Converts color to shaded gray
Filter: wave	Creates wave shapes with an object
Filter: xray	Grayscale color, similar to a x-ray image
Filter: invert	Creates the negative or opposite site of the color number
Filter: mask	Shifts from transparent to specified color

CSS positions can be…
- Relative: using properties ratite(X), top, bottom, right and left.
- Fixed: the same absolute except the parent will be the browser.
- Absolute: the real, absolute given position.
- Static: the default option all elements will be in during normal flow.

Example: 3.5
1. <!DOCTYPE HTML PUBLIC "-//W3C//DTD HTML 4.01//EN"
2. "http://www.w3.org/TR/html4/Strict.dtd">
3. <head>
4. <meta http-equiv="Content-Type" content="text/html; charset=iso-8859-1">
5. <title>CSS Shadows</title>
6. <style type="text/css">
7. <!--

8.   span {
9.   display:inline-block; width:350; height:30;
10. font-size:30px; font-family:arial;
11. color:#000000; font-weight:bold;
12. filter:shadow(color=#daa520,direction=225)
13. }
14. img{
15. position: relative;
16. width:100px; height:70px;
17. left:10px; top:10px
18. filter:shadow(color=#daa520,
       direction=225)
19. -->
20. </style> </head> <body> <p>
21. <img src="C:\\dog.jpg" ALT=
       "Shadowing an image!">
22. <span> Text in Shadow</span>
23. </p> </body>
24. </HTML>

Note: in Internet Explorer (IE) use **display:inline-block;** otherwise you may not get the exact result.

You can see the pleasing effect without using any graphical application. Both the text and the image are shadowed by 225. The 225 is the default effect. Here, we will try to examine more CSS effects.

Shadow position effect

The shadow position effect is quit simple. It works **clockwise**, with the zero on the top of the page and 180 at the bottom.

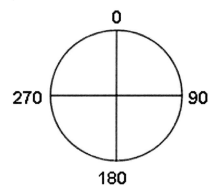

0 = Top
90 = Right
180 = Bottom
225 = Bottom left is
the default option
270 = Left

The 45 is top right, the 320 is top left, and so on.
On line 9 the color is set to #000000, which means black (text color).
The shadow takes two values: the shadow color and the direction.

Alpha effect
Make object blend.
Opacity can be from zero (transparent) to 100 (fully opaque).
Style makes the shape of opacity, such as with the following:
0 = uniform
1 = linear
2 = radial
3 = rectangular
StartX and **startY** means begin on X and Y. On the other hand, the **finishX** and **finishY**
mean the end which is oppose the start.

Example: 3.6

```
1.  <!DOCTYPE HTML PUBLIC "-//W3C//DTD HTML 4.01//EN"
2.  "http://www.w3.org/TR/html4/Strict.dtd">
3.  <head>
4.  <meta http-equiv="Content-Type" content="text/html; charset=iso-8859-1">
5.  <title>Alpha</title>
6.  <style type="text/css">
7.  <!--
8.  span
9.  {
10. display:inline-block;
11. width:250; height:30; font-size:30px;
12. font-family:arial; color:# 000000;
13. font-weight:bold;
14. filter:alpha(Opacity=80,
        FinishOpacity=10, Style=3,
15. StartX=20, StartY=0, FinishX=0,
        FinishY=0)
16. }

17. -->
18. </style></head>
```

19. <body> <p>
20. <img src="C:\\dog.jpg" width=150 height=100 style="filter:alpha(Opacity=100, FinishOpacity=0,Style=2, StartX=30, StartY=50,FinishX=0, FinishY=0)" ALT="Alpha Image!">
21. <span> Alpha Mode</span> </p>
22. </body>
23. </HTML>

Blur effect

To create an image with a little blur, you need to use the CSS blur effect. The *add* means true or false. If added to blur it is *true,* otherwise is is false. The strength is **5px** by default unless you change it to a higher strength value.

<img src="dog.jpg" width="150" height="100"
style="Filter: Blur(Add = 0, Direction = 225, Strength = 8)">
span{
display:inline-block;
width:250; height:30;font-size:30px;
font-family:arial;color:# 000000;
font-weight:bold;Filter: Blur(Add = 1,   Direction = 225,
Strength = 15)}

FlipH & FlipV
The flip effect can flip text horizontally, flipH, or vertically, flipV.

<img src="dog.jpg" width="150" height="100"
style="filter:fliph">
Span{ filter:fliph}

filter:flipv
<img src="dog.jpg" width="120" height="90"
style="filter:flipv">

Wave effect
Freq= frequency of wave
Strength = density
Light= strength of light on the wave motion (0-100)
Phase=sine wave degree (0-100)

Wave effect
You can see the effect of the wave with this simple example.

```
<img src="dog.jpg" width="120" height="90"
style="filter:Wave(Add=0, Freq=1, lightStrength=25,
Phase=90, Strength=10)">
```

More effects
There are more effects you can try. Look at all the rest.
- filter:xray
- filter:mask(color=#cccccc)
- filter:invert
- filter:gray
- filter:glow(color=#000000, strength=5)
- filter:dropshadow(color=#cccccc, offx=5, offy=9)
offx=number of drop shadow along X
offy=number of drop shadow along Y

filter:gray

filter:xray

filter:invert

filter:glow(color=#00ff00, strength=10)

 **filter:dropshadow(color=#cccccc, offx=5, offy=9)**

Laboratory exercises

1- Implement all of these CSS features
1. Create a layout that satisfies all of the following conditions:
2. Create a link "load Image".
3. There must not be a bar under the link.
4. When the mouse is placed on the link, the color becomes red, font becomes 16pt and bars display on the top and bottom.
5. When user clicks, an image (any image) will display on the screen. The image must Flip Vertically.
6. The name of your image must be in shadow format with different colors.

2-Create an external file in CSS that only contains a designed header. Call it *header.css*. Create a webpage that has a link from page2 to page3. When you click on any page, the same header should show. On page1 (the main page), create an overflow box with a scroll that will output a message.

3-Create a webpage. When your webpage has loaded, you should see an image (it could be any image, such as a cat). When the user clicks on the image once, it should Flip Horizontally. The second time, the image should Flip Vertically. By the third click, it should become blurry, and by the fourth click, the image should be wavy.

Chapter 4

CSS Layouts and Menus

Introduction
In addition to image manipulation, CSS has many advanced features that allow us to create very interesting designs. With mouse-over, or *hover*, you can invoke the border of an object to changed as the mouse touches the object. The opacity plays an important role. Automatic image enlargement is also done by CSS. This chapter will also demonstrate transparency and the process of creating a box on the top of background. The most important part of this chapter is the implementation of the menu. We will try to show different menus both horizontally and vertically.

Effect of Mouse on button
One of the interesting features of CSS is its ability to change the behavior of the button when the button is linked to a webpage. The **hover** keyword is used in order to perform this feature.

Border effect
Hover can have an effect on the border or the position of a button. First, you must define your style in CSS and then apply it on the html code.

```
  .bordering img
  {
border: 2px solid red;
 }
  .bordering:hover img
  {
  border: 3px solid blue;
  }
```

The **.bordering img** defines the solid static border, as the webpage is loaded. It will be displayed with a red colored border. The second part (in the shaded area), **.bordering:hover img**, is displayed when the user places a mouse on the link, and will change automatically according to the declared CSS style (the border becomes blue and thicker).

Example: 4.1

1. <!DOCTYPE HTML PUBLIC "-//W3C//DTD HTML 4.01//EN"
2. "http://www.w3.org/TR/html4/Strict.dtd">
3. <head>
4. <meta http-equiv="Content-Type" content="text/html; charset=iso-8859-1">
5. <title>Image Border Effect</title>
6. <style type="text/css" media="screen">
7. <!--
8. .bordering img{
9. border: 2px solid red; }
10. .bordering:hover img {
11. border: 3px solid blue; }
12. -->

If you place a mouse on top of the image, you will see the color of the border automatically change to solid blue.

13. </style></head>
14. <body> <p>
15. <a href="http://www.shanbedi.com"
16. class="bordering"><img src="c:\\button2.jpg" width="80" Alt="CSS Border Effect"></a>
17. </p> </body>
18. </HTML>

More button effects

You may want to change the position of a button when the user puts the mouse on the top of the link, or you may be interested in making the button disappear during mouse activities.

When the mouse touches the link, the position of the button will change to 100px from the left, and the size of the button will become 100px in width.	.bordering img{
	border: 2px solid red;}
	.bordering:hover img{
	border: 3px solid blue;
	position: relative;
	left:100px; width:100px; }

As the mouse touches the button, it will disappear from the page.	.bordering img{
	border: 2px solid red;}
	.bordering:hover img{
	border: 3px solid blue; **display:none}**

Image link opacity

The opacity of an image significantly changes how a user sees that image. We can manipulate alpha-opacity in order to change the transparency of an image. The opacity of an image will change when the user places the mouse on top of it. The **onmouseover** keyword is used when the mouse is placed on the image. The **onmouseout** keyword is used when the mouse is out of the image territory.

Example: 4.2

```
1.  <!DOCTYPE HTML PUBLIC "-//W3C//DTD HTML 4.01//EN"
2.  "http://www.w3.org/TR/html4/Strict.dtd">
3.  <head>
4.  <meta http-equiv="Content-Type" content="text/html; charset=iso-8859-1">
5.  <title>Transparency</title>
6.  <style type="text/css" media="screen">
7.  <!--
8.  img {
9.  filter : alpha(opacity=50); /* for IE  browser*/
10. -moz-opacity: 0.5; /* For Mozilla */
11. }
12. -->
13. </style> </head> <body>
14. <h4>Image Opacity</h4> <p>
15. <a href="http://www.shanbedi.com"> <img
        src="C:\\flower.jpg" Alt= "Image with Opacity!"
        width="100" height="80"
16. onmouseover="filters.alpha.opacity=100"
17. onmouseout="filters.alpha.opacity=30"> </a>
18. </p>
19. </body></html>
```

If you experience any problems with Mozilla then you may use this line:
Onmouseout ="this.style.MozOpacity=0.5; this.filters.alpha.opacity=50"
The value for **Mozilla** is 0 to 1, while for **IE** it is 0 to 100.
What happens if you change the opacity from (**30 to 0**) on line 17?
When *mouseover* the object it will be visible with full Opacity and when the *mouseout* the object it will be vanished from the screen.

Automatic image resizing

Image enlargement is one of the most interesting parts of CSS. Here we do not design anything related to the position of the image. You will see that when the page is first loaded, the image is 100px. Through using mouse-over, the image becomes 200px in width and after mouse-out, it returns to 70px in width.

Example: 4.3

```
1.   <!DOCTYPE HTML PUBLIC "-//W3C//DTD HTML 4.01//EN"
2.   "http://www.w3.org/TR/html4/Strict.dtd">
3.   <head>
4.   <meta http-equiv="Content-Type" content="text/html; charset=iso-8859-1">
5.   <title>Automatic Enlargement</title>
6.   <style type="text/css" media="screen">
7.   </style>
8.   </head>
9.   <body>
10.  <p>
11.  <img src="C:\\donkey.jpg"style= "width:
       100px;"
12.  onmouseover="this.style.width= '200px'
       "
13.  onmouseout="this.style.width=' 70px'  "
       >
14.  </p>
15.  </body>
16.  </html>
```

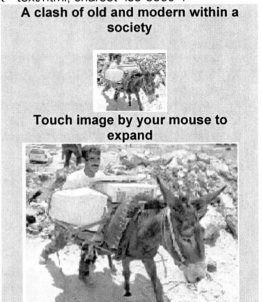

A clash of old and modern within a society

Touch image by your mouse to expand

This is a *simple automatic image* enlargement. We use **onmouseover** for when the mouse is placed on top of the image and **onmouseout** when the mouse moves out of the image area. As the image is touched by mouse, the *width* size becomes 200px. The image returns to the normal size when the mouse leaves the image area.

Positioning enlargement

In the above example, the image enlargement has not been properly positioned. We have to design a CSS style and then apply it to the body of the program. Look at this example which outputs the same as the above example.

Example: 4.4

```
1.   <!DOCTYPE HTML PUBLIC "-//W3C//DTD HTML 4.01//EN"
2.   "http://www.w3.org/TR/html4/Strict.dtd">
3.   <head>
4.   <meta http-equiv="Content-Type" content="text/html; charset=iso-8859-1">
5.   <title>Positioning Enlargement</title>
6.   <style type="text/css" media="screen">
7.   <!--
8.   .Pic span{
9.   position: absolute;   background-color: #FFCC00;
10.  padding: 2px; left:150;  top:30;   visibility: hidden; }
```

11. .Pic:hover span{   visibility: visible; }
12. -->
13. </style> </head> <body> <p>
14. <a class="Pic" href="http://www.shanbedi.com">
15. <img src="C:\\donkey.jpg" Alt="positioning an image!" width="80px" height="50px" >
16. <span><img src="C:\\donkey.jpg" Alt="positioning an image!" width="400" >
    </span></a> </p>
17. </body>
18. </html>

You see the background color that the image will be placed on. **Padding: 2px** indicates the size of padding around the image. The **position: absolute**; means that the top and left values are defined for enlargement. We define the enlargement size as 400 in width.

CSS layers

Layers are boxes or texts that can be placed one over another. In fact, color plays a really important role in layer building. Netscape may act differently regarding the layer layout. To create a layer, simply define the position (whether absolute or relative) and assign some values to the top and left of the layer. The **z-index** identifies which layer can be on the top. The layer with the bigger z-index number will be on the top.   There is no specific purpose for using layers, so every designer uses layers differently and for different reasons.

Example: 4.5

1.   <!DOCTYPE HTML PUBLIC "-//W3C//DTD HTML 4.01//EN"
2.   "http://www.w3.org/TR/html4/Strict.dtd">
3.   <head>
4.   <meta http-equiv="Content-Type" content="text/html; charset=iso-8859-1">
5.   <title>CSS Layers</title>
6.   <style type="text/css" media="screen">
7.   <!--
8.   h2 {
9.   position: relative;
10. top: 25px; left: 70px; z-index: 2;
11. background-color: #4169e1;
12. color: red; width:140px; height:120px;
13. overflow: hidden
14. }
15. div {
16. position: relative;
17. top:-50px; left:50; z-index: 1;
18. background-color: #bdb76b;
19. width:200px; height:120px; overflow: scroll
20. }
21. -->

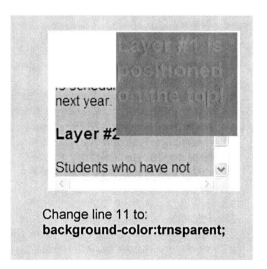

Change line 11 to:
background-color:trnsparent;

22. </style> </head>
23. <body>
24. <h2 >
25. Layer #1 is positioned on the top!
26. </h2>
27. <div>
28. The layer number 2:

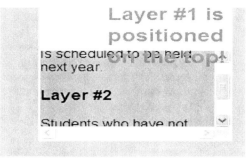

29. The final exam for winter term is scheduled to be held next year.
30. <h3> Layer #2 </h3> Students who have not learned this course properly may still delay the final examination!
31. </div> </body>
32. </html>

Transparency

Box transparency is a way to design the website. Sometimes you may want to create a popup menu that displays transparently. If you want to show some content and, at the same time have the page background be visible, then the box transparency is the best. Transparency is easy in CSS: you just set the **opacity** to the desired values. Once again, for **IE** the range is (0-100) and for **Mozilla** is (0-10).

Example: 4.6

1. <!DOCTYPE HTML PUBLIC "-//W3C//DTD HTML 4.01//EN"
2. "http://www.w3.org/TR/html4/Strict.dtd">
3. <head>
4. <meta http-equiv="Content-Type" content="text/html; charset=iso-8859-1">
5. <title>Transparent Layers</title>
6. <style type="text/css" media="screen">
7. <!--
8. div.back {
9. width: 400px;   height: 250px; border: 1px groove;
10. background: url(c:\\deer.jpg) repeat; }
11. span.box {
12. display:inline-block; /* needed for IE*/
13. width: 300px; height: 200px; margin: 10px 30px;
14. background-color: #f8f8ff; border: 2px solid red;
15. -moz-opacity:0.5; /*For Mozilla*/
16. filter:alpha(opacity=50); /*For IE*/
17. font-weight: bold;font-size:18px;
18. color: #000000; }
10.   >
20. </style> </HEAD> <body> <h2>Transparency</h2>
21. <p> The transparent box allows you
22. </p> <div class="back"> <span class="box">
23. to message out an important thing

24. related to your website while you still
25. see the background of the page.
26. </span> </div> </body>
27. </html>

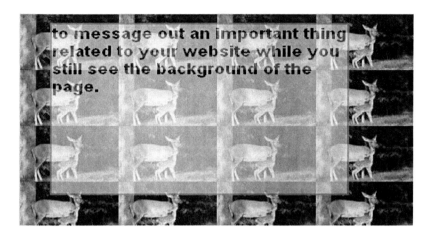

The box is surrounded by a red 2px border and is, therefore, fairly visible.

Menus

In modern layout design many webmasters use a menu, whether horizontal or vertical. The **horizontal** menus line up on a linear array which is clickable and linked to the related pages. The vertical menus are usually placed on the left or right in the navigating bar of the webpage. Menus sometimes contain submenus. There are several ways to create a menu. Some menus are loaded as image files.

Menus in HTML are usually done by using a table. In CSS you may AVOID using tables. In spite their sophistication the table also has some major problems.

Java CSS HTML   **Horizontal Menu**

HTML Easy Web Design
CSS Easy Web Design   **Vertical Menu**
AJAX Easy Web Design
PHP Easy Web Design

Simple menus

CSS has the ability to generate different menus. There are two types of simple menus: a horizontal menu which is placed on the head of the page and a vertical menu which is usually placed on the right or left side of the page. The color of the menu plays a significant role.

Horizontal menu

The horizontal menu is more clear and visible simply because it placed on the top of the page. It is preferable when the size of the menu caption is precise.

Example: 4.7

```
1.   <!DOCTYPE HTML PUBLIC "-//W3C//DTD HTML 4.01//EN"
2.   "http://www.w3.org/TR/html4/Strict.dtd">
3.   <head>
4.   <meta http-equiv="Content-Type" content="text/html; charset=iso-8859-1">
5.   <title>Horizontal Menu</title>
6.   <style type="text/css" media="screen">
7.   <!--
8.   td.tb1 {
9.   background: #FFCC00;
10.  font-size:16px;     font-weight: bold;
11.  }
12.  td.tb2 {
13.  background: #999999;
14.  font-size:16px; font-weight: bold;
15.  }
16.  -->
17.  </style></head>   <body>
18.  <table  cellpadding="3" >
19.  <tr><td class="tb1"> HTML </td>
20.  <td class="tb2">CSS </td>
21.  <td class="tb1">AJAX </td>
22.  <td class="tb2">
23.  PHP </td> </tr> </table> </body>
24.  </html>
```

HTML CSS AJAX PHP

The caption of each cell is precise. The background color is different, so it will be more visible.

You will see that instead of "HTML Easy Design", we just use a short text caption like "HTML"

Vertical menu

The vertical menu is preferable when the length of the text is a little longer than just one word. For example, instead of just typing HTML, you may want to use the full name like *HTML Easy Web Design*.

Example: 4.8

```
1.   <!DOCTYPE HTML PUBLIC "-//W3C//DTD HTML 4.01//EN"
2.   "http://www.w3.org/TR/html4/Strict.dtd">
3.   <head>
4.   <meta http-equiv="Content-Type" content="text/html; charset=iso-8859-1">
```

5. <title>Vertical Menu</title>
6. <style type="text/css" media="screen">
7. <!--
8. tr.tb1 {
9. background: #FFCC00; font-size:16px; font-weight: bold;
10. }
11. tr.tb2 {
12. background: #999999; font-size:16px; font-weight: bold;
13. }
14. -->
15. </style> </head> <body>
16. <table width="200" cellpadding="3" >
17. <tr class="tb1"><td>
18. HTML Easy Web Design</td>
19. </tr> <tr class="tb2"><td>
20. CSS Easy Web Design</td>
21. </tr> <tr class="tb1"><td>
22. AJAX Easy Web Design</td>
23. <tr class="tb2"><td>
24. PHP Easy Web Design</td>
25. </tr> </table> </body> </html>

HTML Easy Web Design
CSS Easy Web Design
AJAX Easy Web Design
PHP Easy Web Design

The cellpadding ="3" creates spaces between each menu bar.

Automatic highlighting background

Onmouseover =" this.className and **onmouseout** = "this.className = 'tb1'" changes the background according to the pre-set background. We can use hover for this is simple background manipulation because it provides better functionalities.

Example: 4.9
1. <!DOCTYPE HTML PUBLIC "-//W3C//DTD HTML 4.01//EN"
2. "http://www.w3.org/TR/html4/Strict.dtd">
3. <head>
4. <meta http-equiv="Content-Type" content="text/html; charset=iso-8859-1">
5. <title>Automatic Highlighting</title>
6. <style type="text/css" media="screen">
7. <!--
8. td.tb1 { background: #FFCC00; font-size:16px; font-weight: bold; }
9. td.tb2 { background: #999999; font-size:16px; font-weight: bold; }
10. -->
11. </style> </head> <body> <table cellpadding="6" >
12. <tr><td class="tb1" onmouseover="this.className='tb2' "
13. onmouseout="this.className ='tb1'">HTML </td>
14. <td class="tb1" onmouseover="this.className='tb2'"
15. onmouseout="this.className='tb1'">CSS </td></tr>
16. </table> </body> </html>

HTML CSS

Just put your mouse on the above button and see how the background of button is changed.

Vertical background change
The <UL> and <LI> styles provide better menus compared to what a table can do. Here you do not need to create a table. The reality is that all menus are linked to some websites or files, so we can change the behavior of the hover, link, active and visited, etc.

Example: 4.10

```
1.  <!DOCTYPE HTML PUBLIC "-//W3C//DTD HTML 4.01//EN"
2.  "http://www.w3.org/TR/html4/Strict.dtd">
3.  <head>
4.  <meta http-equiv="Content-Type" content="text/html; charset=iso-8859-1">
5.  <title>Automatic Highlighting</title>
6.  <style type="text/css" media="screen">
7.  <!--
8.  td.tb1 {
9.  background: #FFCC00;
10. font-size:16px; font-weight: bold;
11. height: 25px; width:200px;
12. border: ridge yellow;
13. }
14. td.tb2 {
15. background: #999999;
16. font-size:16px; font-weight: bold;
17. height: 30px;width:250px;
18. border: ridge yellow; text-align:center;
19. }
20. -->
21. </style> </head> <body> <table  cellpadding="6" >
22. <tr><td class="tb1" onmouseover="this.className='tb2' "
23. onmouseout="this.className ='tb1'">HTML and CSS </td></tr>
24. <tr> <td class="tb1" onmouseover="this.className='tb2'"
25. onmouseout="this.className='tb1'">PHP and MySQL </td></tr>
26. <tr> <td class="tb1" onmouseover="this.className='tb2'"
27. onmouseout="this.className='tb1'"><a href="http://www.dreamweaver.com"
        style="text-decoration:none" >Ajax </a></td></tr>
28. <tr> <td class="tb1" onmouseover="this.className='tb2'"
29. onmouseout="this.className='tb1'"><a href="http://www.JavaScript.com"
        style="text-decoration:none" >JavaScript</a></td></tr>
30. </table> </body>
31. </html>
```

When you put the mouse on the menu link, the background color will automatically change and also watch another two changes, the text caption moves to the center and button size will enlarge.

You can call the menu by <div id="menu"> and use <UL> in order to output the bullets beside the menu. Here we made the border a little thicker in order to be more visible. You can use a tiny border which also looks nice!

- HTML Easy Web Design
- CSS Easy Web Design
- AJAX Easy Web Design
- PHP Easy Web Design
- JAVA Advanced Web Design
- JSP Advanced Web Design

```
<div id="menu">
<ul>
<li><a href="#" >JAVA </a></li>
<li><a href="#" >JSP  </a></li>
</ul>
<div>
```

You may want to have an "angle quotation mark (right)" right in front of the menu caption, so you can use "**»**" and we use "** **" in order to have some spaces after the " **»** "HTML entity.

» HTML Easy Web Design

» CSS Easy Web Design

» JavaScript Easy Web Design

» AJAX Easy Web Design

» PHP Easy Web Design

» JAVA Advanced Web Design

» JSP Advanced Web Design

```
<ul id="menu">
<li><a href="#"> &raquo;   HTML
Easy Web Design</a></li>
<li><a    href="#"    >&raquo; CSS
Easy Web Design</a></li>
</ul>
```

Menu buttons

Attaching images in CSS is mostly done by using a background or a background-image such as **background-image: url(menu1.gif);**, where the menu1.gif is the file name. In order to see a different menu or a different color, you must use hover which will invoke another image to load, as with **background-image:url(menu2.gif);**. In this instance, the two files, **menu1.gif** and **menu2.gif**, are the exactly same; they differ only in color

In the above example, if you shrink the margin by using negative numbers then you will see this nice looking menu: **_Margin: -18px;_**

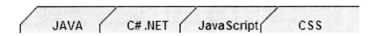

Example: 4.11
1. <!DOCTYPE HTML PUBLIC "-//W3C//DTD HTML 4.01//EN"
2. "http://www.w3.org/TR/html4/Strict.dtd">
3. <head>
4. <meta http-equiv="Content-Type" content="text/html; charset=iso-8859-1">
5. <title>buttons background</title>
6. <style type="text/css" media="screen">
7. <!--
8. .menu a{
9. text-decoration: none; font: bold 12px Arial; color: black;
10. width: 100px; height: 20px; float:left; margin-right: 0px;
11. background-image:url(**C:\\menu2.gif**);
12. background-repeat: no-repeat;
13. padding-top: 12px; text-align:center; }
14. .menu a:hover{
15. background-image:url(**C:\\menu1.gif**); }
16. -->
17. </style> </head>
18. <body>
19. <div class="menu">
20. <a href="#">JAVA </a> <a href="#">C# .NET </a>
21. <a href="#">JavaScript </a> <a href="#">CSS</a>
22.

23. </div><h4>Welcome to background Images</h4>
24. </body>
25. </html>

Vertical menu button

In the previous example we created a horizontal button menu by loading an image. Now we want to do the same thing, but this time with vertical menus in which images are displayed vertically. First the **float: left** has to be removed because it is used for horizontal menus. In vertical menus, we use the <UL> which is the best option to create a vertical menu. Wherever there is a problem with the **<LI>** tag, it simply outputs a bullet in front of each image. You need to use **UL { list-style:none; }** in order to remove this bullet.

Example: 4.12

```
1.  <!DOCTYPE HTML PUBLIC "-//W3C//DTD HTML 4.01//EN"
2.  "http://www.w3.org/TR/html4/Strict.dtd">
3.  <head>
4.  <meta http-equiv="Content-Type" content="text/html; charset=iso-8859-1">
5.  <title>Buttons background</title>
6.  <style type="text/css" media="screen">
7.  <!--
8.  .menu a{
9.  display:inline-block;
10. text-decoration: none;
11. font: bold 12px Arial;  color: black;
12. width: 150px; height: 20px;  margin-right: 5px;
13. background-image:url(C:\\menu1.gif);
14. background-repeat: no-repeat;
15. padding-top: 10px; text-align:center; }
16. .menu a:hover {
17. background-image:url(C:\\menu2.gif);
18. }
19. Ul { list-style:none; }
20. -->
21. </style></head>    <body>
22. <ul class="menu">
23. <li><a href="#">JAVA
        Programming</a></li>
24. <li><a href="#">C# .NET </a></li>
25. <li><a href="#">JavaScript </a></li>
26. <li><a href="#">CSS Web Design</a></li>
27. </UL>
28. </body>
29. </html>
```

You can use any other image.

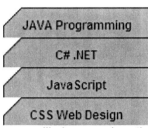

The image will change when the user places the mouse on it. First, the menu1.gif will appear and then the menu2.gif file will display because of **hover**.

If you remove line 8 "**background-image:url(menu1.gif);** ", the image will load and you will only see the text. The image menu2.gif is activated by placing a mouse on the text.

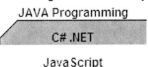

JavaScript

CSS Web Design

Laboratory exercises

1-Create a webpage which upon loading, an image will show on the screen. Use an image of a goat, sized 100 X 100. When the user puts the mouse on the image, it should automatically enlarge to 200 X 200 and, instead of being a goat, it should change into a camel.

2- Design a simple page with a nice background. On the top of the page, use a red layer to write, "Welcome to my site". Make another blue layer on the top half of the layer in order to write "See Yahoo page". Load an image inside the webpage. When you put your mouse on the image, its opacity will change automatically. Use any density for the opacity.

3-Design a nice layout containing both horizontal and vertical menus. On the horizontal menu use some button images with these captions: Home, Tutorials, **Ajax** and **Java**, which will change color upon using mouse-over. Place your vertical menu on the left (20%). The menus are set vertically and, by putting a mouse on any of the menus, they should become shadowy or display a button.

Part II
JavaScript

This part of book covers the JavaScript form the beginning. It provides brief definition along with many examples. We display the graphics result for each example, so students get some ideas about the result of the code even before running the examples.

Chapter 5

Introduction to JavaScript

Introduction

JavaScript was developed by Netscape to handle interactive WebPages in ways not possible by using the pure HTML. With JavaScript you can easily do calculation by using textboxes, and enter your desired values to calculate according to your formula. It can validate the forms (data validation) and write a programming script that accomplishes your demand. JavaScript is very easy to learn and to understand, however it has ability to perform very complex programming features. JavaScript, as the name implies, is a scripting language, which means it does not need to be compiled before execution, the same way that the C++ or Java language does. In this chapter we will look at some simple understanding of JavaScript which prepare you for further studies. In this chapter we bring up the most fundamental understanding of JavaScript and you will become familiar with the basic syntax of JavaScript code.

What is JavaScript?

- ▶ JavaScript is a scripting language
- ▶ JavaScript is adding interactivity to the HTML
- ▶ In spite of great performance, it is easy to learn
- ▶ JavaScript consists of codes the same as C/C++ and JAVA languages but not hard like C/C++ and JAVA.
- ▶ JavaScript can be directly embedded into HTML
- ▶ JavaScript is a powerful scripting language for designing web pages
- ▶ You can use JavaScript to validate data
- ▶ JavaScript is designed perfectly to deal with the **client-side**

History of JavaScript

Netscape was the first Java licensee to allow a Java applet to be run under the Netscape version 2. JavaScript was originally developed by Brendan Eich of Netscape Communications Corporation under the name *Mocha*, then renamed to LiveScript, and finally given the official name JavaScript. JavaScript was first introduced in the Netscape browser version 2.0 in 1995. Microsoft Internet Explorer made it possible for JavaScript to be run under IE. It is officially called "JScript" because Netscape owns the name "JavaScript". Today JavaScript is very popular and usable among many web developers. It can be very complex if you want to do very complex tasks with JavaScript.

Client-side

The **client-side** is simply the website that you are visiting on the Internet (websites). If you try to buy a book from Amazon.com then you need to fill out the form with your personal information, and this means you work on the client-side. When you press the submit button this means you are sending your information to the server-side. The server-side echoes an answer back to you which it messages out as a conformation form.

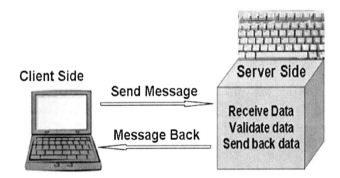

JavaScript vs. HTML

HTML is the basic script for Web design. It is limited to static web pages therefore it can not perform the dynamic client-side operations. In order to have dynamic web pages you need some script programming that performs dynamically. JavaScript is in high demand for today's web designing. In order to simplify the JavaScript you need HTML.

JavaScript vs. Java

Note: JavaScript is not the same as Java. Again: JavaScript is not the Java language.

JavaScript is designed for use within HTML and capable of building websites: it is scripting language. JavaScript is used in almost every type of Web design due to its great abilities. Java language is a real programming language. It is very powerful language that performs excellently in all programming dimensions. Java is developed by the company

SUN Microsystems and it is different from JavaScript. Today Java language is the most usable language for Medicine, Science, Engineering, Internet, Networking and the like. JavaScript is a powerful client-side language. Everything you see front of you on the website is classified as client-side.

| JavaScript is easy to learn while Java language is a little hard to learn ||
JavaScript Language	Java language
Compilation: No need for compilation	Need to be compiled before execution
Need browser to run	Can be run as stand alone
Program installation needed	Install JDK
Easy script language	Complex language
Interface: HTML	Interface: AWT or Swing
Many commands like:, if, else, while are the same as java	********************

HTML

HTML is known as the basis of all website designs. It is easy to learn and you certainly need some knowledge of HTML in order to study JavaScript. We try to bring some of most the needed features of HTML into the next chapter. HTML is the core of a web page. HTML is static. None of its tags can change once the page has been loaded. JavaScript can make your pages dynamic and interactive. However, if you already are familiar with HTML then you may skip the chapter.

The simple HTML code is similar to this:

<HTML>
Body of the page
</HTML>

Example: 5.1

```
<html>
<head>
<title>Title of page</title>
</head>
<body>
<b>Hello this is my webpage.</b> <br> this page is in pure HTML!
</body>
</html>
```

The above code produces this website.

Embedded HTML

JavaScript needs to be embedded into HTML therefore you need to be familiar with HTML. Look at how JavaScript is embedded into HTML:

```
<html>
<body>
<script type="text/javascript">
</script>
</body>
</html>
```

You see the tag **<script type="text/javascript"> </script>**
JavaScript is embedded into an HTML tag.

Now look at the **Syntax of JavaScript**

Example: 5.2
```
<html>
<body>
<script type="text/JavaScript">
document.write("This is my webpage!")
</script>
</body>
</html>
```

The **document.write()** function is the JavaScript function that handle strings.
Look at the two outputs from HTML and JavaScript.

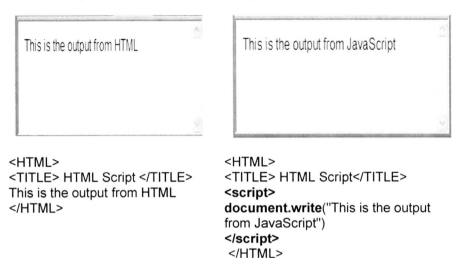

```
<HTML>
<TITLE> HTML Script </TITLE>
This is the output from HTML
</HTML>
```

```
<HTML>
<TITLE> HTML Script</TITLE>
<script>
document.write("This is the output
from JavaScript")
</script>
 </HTML>
```

CSS and JavaScript

As we mentioned earlier there are three script languages of web design that has to pay attention considerably. HTML is used for contents of the pages, CSS is about design and creating nice layout and finally JavaScript allows you to create dynamic and interactive WebPages. In fact we combine all three parts in order to create good website.

The Three Important Parts

To build dynamic websites you need to have some knowledge of the client-side, the server-side, and databases. For the client-side you may use JavaScript, for the server side you may want to use PHP and most likely to handle your data in the database you use **MySQL**. You can use Oracle, **SQL** Server, MySQL or any other suitable database. MySQL and PHP are most useable in today's internet, both are free and you can download PHP or download MySQL to work with. After you completed this book you will probably need to learn PHP+MySQL.

Web Design Tools

Adobe Dreamweaver is a Web development application which was created by **Macromedia**. Dreamweaver can be run under both Mac and Windows. The recent versions support new technologies such as CSS and JavaScript. Dreamweaver is a tool, therefore instead of writing code from the beginning to end you just click on the option tools. The code will be generated automatically. It helps developers to design their web pages but there are some downsides to using web application tools.

For one, it produces code that is very big and the file size and amount of HTML code is much larger than it should be, therefore browsers perform poorly. So the best way to create web pages is to write code from the ground up. If you use Web design tools then you may need to clean up some unnecessary code generated by the tool.

Macromedia Flash: Flash is one of the more interesting web design tools. Usually it is used to create animations. When you develop your web design you may need to know about using Flash. Adobe Flash Professional is used to create content web applications, games and movies, and even for mobile phones and other embedded devices.

Adobe Photoshop: This program is really great for creating graphics. When you develop your web pages you probably need to know how to modify your website images.

What is W3C

W3C was created in October 1994 by Tim Berners-Lee, inventor of the Web. **W3C** stands for the World Wide Web Consortium (WWW) and it is working to standardize the Web. The most recommendations for web design come from W3C.

W3C is hosted by these three universities:
- ▶ Massachusetts Institute of Technology in the USA
- ▶ The French National Research Institute in Europe
- ▶ Keio University in Japan

Browser support

A **web browser** is a software application that enables users to display text, images, videos, and music in different file formats and interact with multimedia. There are different kinds of browser therefore they respond to the objects differently. As a web developer you must know how to overcome issues with various browsers. Fortunately, these days almost all browsers act pretty similar. Mozilla **Firefox** and Internet Explorer are the most useable browsers.

Syntax

JavaScript can be easily embedded into HTML code. The syntax is fairly simple. You must open and close a script tag like this:

<SCRIPT> ... </SRIPT>

Assign *JavaScript* to the language like:

<Script language = "JavaScript" > *This is the Netscape* version which has been deprecated by the W3C. You may use this **<Script type = " text/JavaScript" >** however it is suggested that you use both (in case of dealing with older browsers).

By using the above code the browser knows that this part of HTML contains JavaScript, then it has to evaluate it as a JavaScript tag.

Embedding into HTML

There are three ways that JavaScript can be embedded into HTML.
- » Embedded in head section
- » Embedded in body section
- » External JavaScript file

Embedded in the head section

If JavaScript is embedded in the head section of HTML then it guarantees that it will load into the pages before the body.

```
<html>
<head>
<Script Language = "JavaScript">
</Script>
</head>
<body>
</body>
</html>
```

Embedded in the body section

We simply put the script tags into the body of HTML.

```
<html>
<head>
</head>
<body>
<Script Language = "JavaScript">
</Script>
</body>
</html>
```

Simple program

The *document.write()* is the most important method in JavaScript. It is used to output multiple statements. Each statement must be separated by a coma.
Note: Javascript is a case sensitive language, therefore uppercase and lowercase characters are not the same. For example, **d**ocument.write**()** is not the same as **D**ocument.write().
We will start a program that uses **d**ocument.write(). So save the example below as" **Prog1.html** "then open it under the browser.

Example: 5.3

1. <HTML> <HEAD>
2. <TITLE> Simple JavaScript </TITLE>
3. <Script type = " text/JavaScript" >
    document.write (" Output from JavaScript!");
4. </SCRIPT>
5. </HEAD>
6. <body>
7.
Output from HTML!
8. </body>
9. </HTML>

Whoops, wait a minute, why should I use the *document.write()* method, since I can just use simple HTML string? Yes, here you can use HTML code but remember, later you will see the differences. JavaScript is a dynamic language therefore you will see how we call variables, operators and objects, things that are not possible to do using pure HTML code. How to use mathematical functions, user defined functions, conditional statements, loops and so on are not available in simple HTML.

Line break
In JavaScript you can use document.write() or document.writeln(); the difference is that document.write() does not return to the new line while the document.writeln() does. **document.writeln** is the same as **document.write** but adds a new line.

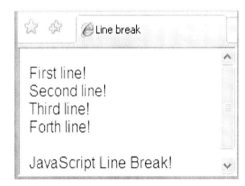

Example: 5.4
1. <HTML> <HEAD>
2. <TITLE> *Line break* </TITLE>
3. </HEAD>
4. <body>
5. <Script type = " text/JavaScript" >
   document.writeln (" First line!
");
6. document.writeln (" Second line!
");
7. document.write (" Third line!
");
8. document.write (" Forth line!
");
9. </SCRIPT>
10.
JavaScript Line Break!
11. </body>
12. </HTML>

Comments
Comments allow you to write some notes to yourself within your program that will not be shown on the browser. In fact, you can describe your function or variables and other elements within your program. Using comments allows you to understand your code especially when you have not been working with it for a relatively long time.

In JavaScript, you can write both one-line comments and multiple-line comments. For a one-line comment you use these double slashes, "*//*", which cover only one line of code. The multiple-line comments cover several lines or even the entire code. Use this sign for the multiple-line:
 / comments */.*

Example: 5.5
1. <HTML> <HEAD>
2. <TITLE> Comments </TITLE>
3. </HEAD> <body>
4. <Script type = " text/JavaScript" >
   *//document.writeln (" Single line comment: This line will not be shown!
");*
5. document.writeln (" I am not commented out!
 So you see me!
");
6. */*document.write (" Comment out by multiple*

7. document.write (" Comment out by multiple line!
");*/
8. </SCRIPT>
9.
Last two lines are under multiple line comments!
10.   </body>
11.   </HTML>

Line 7 is the single-line comment and lines 9 and 10 are both under the multiple-line comments

Browser issue

If a browser does not understand the <SCRIPT> tag, it will skip over it and print out the entire code as ordinary text. You must prevent this from happening. We use the characters **<!--** after the <SCRIPT> tag had been declared and use the characters **-->** before the </SCRIPT> tag is closed. By using this, a non-JavaScript supported browser (old browsers) will see it as a comment and will not print it out.

The simplest JavaScript program looks like this:

1. <script type="text/javascript">
2. **<!--** *to hide script contents from old browsers*
3. document.write("The simple JavaScript syntax!")
4. *// ending line 2* **-->**
5. </script>

Example: 5.6

1.   <HTML> <HEAD>
2.   <TITLE> Browser Compatibility </TITLE> </HEAD>
3.   <body>
      <Script type = " text/JavaScript" >
      <!-- *hide from old browser*
4.   document.writeln ("Old browser version does not display this line!");
            -->
5.   </SCRIPT>
6.   </body>
7.   </HTML>

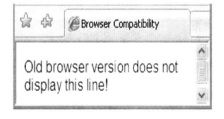

Ending with a Semicolon

JavaScript is smart enough to read a code without a semicolon and turn it correctly. For example these two lines (one with semicolon and one without semicolon) will be the same:

document.wirte("First Prize")   *with no semicolon*
document.wirte("First Prize") ; *with semicolon*

Alert box

JavaScript provides alert boxes that can be used for a quick message. Alert boxes are designed in an elegant format. You can use them for several purposes such as popup, message box, urgent cases, deadline and so on.

The **\r** means carriage return – it returns to the new line.

Example: 5.7
1. <HTML>
2. <HEAD><TITLE> Alert Box </TITLE>
3. </HEAD>
4. <BODY>
5. <script type="text/javascript">
6. <!--
7. **alert**("The registration will end **\r** at 25/DEC/2009! **\r** click OK to see more...")
8. **alert**("Apply for loan by next semester! **\r** click OK to go")
9. -->
10. </script>
11. </BODY>
12. </HTML>

Basic text formatting

JavaScript allows using all HTML tags. Tags like <B>, <I>, <HR> and son can easily be used in JavaScript.

Example: 5.8
1. <HTML>
2. <HEAD><TITLE> Text format </TITLE>
3. </HEAD>
4. <BODY>
5. <script type="text/javascript">
6. **<!--**
7. document.write("<H1><I><font color=blue><center>Welcome to my

site! **</H1> </I> </font> </center>");**
8. document.write("This website is still under construction!");
9. **-->**
10. </script>
11. </BODY>
12. </HTML>

<H1> header big font
<I>   Italic
<font color=blue> return color to blue.

On the above example we made the headline in blue color and the rest of the code in black. The text used some tags like <B>, <I>, <H1>.

Background color

Again, we can use **bgcolor** from the HTML tag to create background color for our website. Look at this example.

The document.write **(" <body bgcolor=yellow>")** turn background color in yellow.

Example: 5.9
1. <HTML>
2. <HEAD> <TITLE> Background color </TITLE>
3. </HEAD>
4. <BODY>
5. **<script language="JavaScript" type= "text/javascript">**
6. <!--
7. document.write(" <body bgcolor=yellow>")
8. document.write("<H1> <I> <font color = blue><center>Welcome to my site!</H1></I></font></center>");
9. document.write ("The page background is in yellow!");
10. -->
11. </script>
12. </BODY>
13. </HTML>

Whoops! Wait a minute: why so we use two script formats like:
<script language="JavaScript" and the **type= "text/javascript">** at the same time? Well, because some older browsers like Netscape are using the
 <script language = " JavaScript" >, and the newer ones are using

<script type="text/javascript">, therefore the best idea is to use both. However these days almost all Internet users are using the newer browsers and the **Firefox** browser is becoming universal (it is very good and free). Therefore there not so many problems exist related to browser incompatibilities.

External JavaScript file

We use external files when we want to use the same script on different pages. The advantage of using external files is that you don't need to rewrite the same code again. You just create a JavaScript file and you call it in every page. Remember the extension of such a file must be "**.js**" and NOT "html".

Example
<html>
<head>
<Script = "**headPage.js**"> </Script>
</head>
<body>
</body>
</html>

Let's create a JavaScript file and call it in several pages. By using external files you save typing time and the document becomes significantly shorter.
Note: the external file must be written in JavaScript and only in JavaScript (pure JavaScript, not html, not script tag).

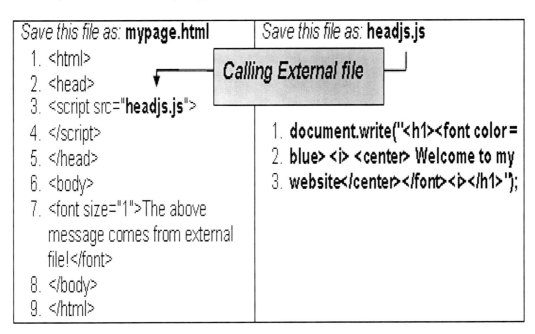

Run the **mypage.html** file to see the web page.

On line 3 the **headjs.js** is called in the *mypage.html* file. Any time you run the mypage.html, it brings up the *headjs.js* (JavaScript file). You can call the headjs.js in every web pages that you like.

NOSCRIPT tag

In spite of browser modernization and the level of availability of new browsers there still may be some users that are using an old browser or who have disabled JavaScript. It is good to use **<noscript>** to send a message in case of an older browser. If Internet users are using an old browser the message comes out from the <NOSCRIPT> tag for them.

Example: 5.10

1. <HTML>
2. <HEAD> <TITLE> NOSCRIPT </TITLE>
3. <script language="JavaScript" type="text/javascript">
        <!--
4. ***LM = document.lastModified ;***
5. document.write("Last modification: "+LM);
        -->
6. </script>
7. </HEAD>
8. <BODY>
9. **<noscript>**
10. Modification was made on Dec/2008
11. **</noscript>**
12. </BODY>
13. </HTML>

Last modification: 12/21/2007 13:51:51

Review questions

1-what is the difference between the **<Script language = "JavaScript" >** and **<Script type = "text/JavaScript" >** forms of declaration?

2- There are three ways that JavaScript can be embedded into HTML; list them all.

3-JavaScript is case sensitive. True   False

4-Why should you use <!—and // --> ON SCRIPT?

5-What does this line in the code do? <Script = "**Mypage.js**"> </Script>

6-The HTML code must not be included in the external file. True False

7- Why do we use <NOSCRIPT> in the code?

8- What does *document.lastModified;* do?

9- How do you use the "return to new line" in JavaScript?

10- How you use the carriage return on the alert box?

Answers

1- **<Script language = "JavaScript" >** this form is Netscape's properties and has been deprecated.

2- The three forms are:
- Embedded in head section
- Embedded in body section
- External file

3- True

4- For older browsers that do not support the new features of JavaScript (*hide from old*)

5- Call external file

6- True

7- if the user has disabled JavaScript then it send the message out to the browser's users.

8- It is a function that prints out the last modification

9- You can use

10- You can use **\r**.

Chapter 6

Data Types

Introduction
The type of data is essential for any programming languages. By declaring the type of data, the compiler knows what type of data has to be dealt with. In JavaScript, we can declare variables the same way as some of the programming languages (Java). However, the JavaScript is known as "loosely typed language," which means you can perform your code without identifying the exact type. In this chapter we learn how about declaring variables, naming variables, working with variables, understanding the literal declaration, using quotation, the rules of Escape sequences, and much more.

Understanding data types
A JavaScript **interpreter** understands two basic data types: numbers and text (**string**). String means a collection of characters, and number can also be called **integer** or **float**. Other types of data can be **Boolean** (true or false), and there is even a type which has no value at all which is called **null**.

First, we must look at basic data types in JavaScript. Suppose you want to add two numbers like 35 and 25: then you use the plus operator"+".

The result of 35 + 25 is 60; or, if you add "Hi" + "JavaScript" the interpreter of JavaScript understands that we want to concatenate the two strings, therefore producing *HiJavaScript*. Check this simple example:

Example: 6.1
```
1.  <!DOCTYPE HTML PUBLIC "-//W3C//DTD HTML 4.01 Transitional//EN"
    "http://www.w3.org/TR/html4/loose.dtd">
2.  <html>
3.  <head>
4.  <title>Basic Data</title>
5.  <meta http-equiv="Content-Type" content="text/html; charset=iso-8859-1">
6.  <script language="JavaScript" type="text/javascript">
7.  document.write("The result of addition:");
```

8.   document.write(35+25 +"<br>");
9.   document.write("The result of concatenation:");
10. document.write("Hi"+" JavaScript"+ "<br>");
11. </script> </head> <body>
12. </body> </html>

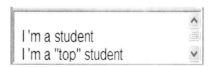

The result of addition:60
The result of concatenation:HiJavaScript

In JavaScript the string has to be placed inside a pair of double quotation marks as in "String", or single quotation marks as in 'String'.

Escape characters

Sometimes you may want to use **slashes** or apostrophes in your string, as in: 'I'm a student'.

In such cases you may encounter some problems, because the JavaScript interpreter sees this punctuation as opening or closing a quotation. The letter I is treated as a letter inside the single quotation, therefore the single quotation at the end of sentence is left an orphan.

document.write('I'm a student'); this line produce no output, it is simply a wrong statement. To fix such a statement you need to use escape characters. What is an escape character? As its name implies, it is used to escape from a compiler or interpreter and consists of a backslash followed by a character.

The code has to be fixed, as in: document.write('I \'m a student'); the letter m is placed inside the escape character.

document.writeln('I \'m a student' + "<br>");
document.writeln('I \'m a "top" student');

I 'm a student
I 'm a "top" student

If you use double quotations then you get the problem:
 document.writeln(" I \'m a "top" student "); it has to be fixed like:
document.writeln(" I \'m a \" top \" student ");

There are several escape characters, look at the list of escape characters in JavaScript.

Escape Sequence	Character
\'	Single quotation mark
\"	Double quotation mark
\\	Backslash
\b	Backspace
\f	Form feed
\n	New line
\r	Carriage return
\t	Tab
\ddd	ddd Octal sequence
\xdd	Hexadecimal sequence

Here are escape characters in the alert box:
**alert('This is Alert box!\r\rThis is the \"Second line!\" \r\tThis is \"Third line!\"\"\r\r
--->the end')**

Working with variables
So far we have worked with string without declaring any variables, but it is not always possible to have code without variables. When we declare variables it means we store the data in the **memory** and the system knows what type of data has to be implemented, so we can use it later. We already mentioned that the data types in JavaScript consist of number, string, Boolean and null.

Declaring variables
Declaring variables is very easy you just need to assign some value to your variable type. Use a semi-colon to show the end of the declaration.

   Y=100;   this is an integer number
   X=21.99 this is a real number
   Z= "Peter Dawson"; this is a string declaration

When you declare Y=100; it means a number of 100 is assigned to the Y, therefore the Y now has value of 100.

- » **Integer**: The integer numbers consist of whole numbers (number with no decimal places) like: -100, -1, 0, 100, 1000 and so on.
- » **Real**: the real numbers are numbers with decimal places such as: -9.99, 10.99, 100.49 and so on.
- » **Character**: the character means a letter. It can be lowercase from (a to z) or uppercase from (A to Z). You can declare number as character (0 t0 9). Put characters in single quotes like this: 'C'.
- » **String**: the String means a collection of characters, as in "I am student".

Example: 6.2

1. `<!DOCTYPE HTML PUBLIC "-//W3C//DTD HTML 4.01 Transitional//EN"`
   `"http://www.w3.org/TR/html4/loose.dtd">`
2. `<html>`
3. `<head>`
4. `<title>Basic Data</title>`
5. `<meta http-equiv="Content-Type" content="text/html; charset=iso-8859-1">`
6. `<script language="JavaScript" type="text/javascript">`
7. `Y = 100;`
8. `X = -99.99;`
9. `Z = " I am stored in the Z";`
10. `document.write('The Y value is: '+Y);`
11. `document.write("<br>"+'The X value is:' +X);`
12. `document.write("<br>"+'The Z value is:' +Z);`
13. `</script>`
14. `</head>`
15. `<body>`
16. `</body>`
17. `</html>`

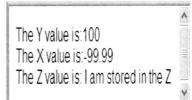

For the purpose of clarity declare a variable using the **var** keyword, followed by a name for the variable, followed by a semi-colon.

var month="April"
var number;
var male=true;   Boolean declaration

Although using the **var** keyword outside of a function is optional it is good practice to always use the **var**. There are however some places where its use is obligatory such as:

» If a global variable with the same name exists.

» If several functions are using variables of the same name.

You may want to use the multiple declarations like this:

var number, X, Y;
or
var price=100, quantity;

Rules of naming variables

There are some rules that have to be respected when you declare the variable name.

» The first character must not be a number like **var 99days;**

» There must not be spaces between name declarations like: **var my name;** but you can use underscores, for example **var my_name;**

» The variable name can't be JavaScript **reserved words**.

» Use a descriptive name for your variable name. For example if you want to declare Class Average, then declare it as *var class_avarage;* Not as *var C_AV;*

» There's no limit to the length of the variable name.

Reserved words

The reserved words are those words that are used as commands in JavaScript, for example if you use **var function;** then the JavaScript interpreter thinks that you have declared a function. The word function is known by the interpreter.

List of reserved words				
break	debugger	for	super	try
case	default	function	switch	typeof
class	else	if	this	void
catch	enum	import	throw	while
const	export	in	true	with
continue	extends	new		
do	false	null		
delete	finally	return		

Initializing variables

When you declare a variable name such as: var number; this declaration is **null**, which means no value is assigned to this variable name. Sometimes you need to initialize the variable and assign some value to the variable, for instance: var number=200;

The most useful declaration is known as literal declaration or **string literal**. When you have "Hello Script" this is string literal, you can assign literal to the variable name like this: var   str ="Hello JavaScript"; then you can use an alert box to see the output, alert (str);

Variable Scope

A variable declared or initialized outside of the function is known as a global variable. The **global** variable is accessible to the entire code (**Global Scope**). If a variable is declared inside the function then it is accessible only to the related function (**Local variable**).

Special Case: If a variable is initialized inside a function body but the keyword of **var** is not declared then this variable has global scope.

Operators

Operators have a special role in programming language; each language might have its own operator. JavaScript uses operators much similar to Java programming. Operators make a program quite manageable. In this chapter we use different types of operators.

Important operators

In this part we introduce several important operators that make JavaScript more dynamic and facilitate the nature of programming.

Arithmetic operators

The basic arithmetic operators perform the simple mathematical actions. The basic arithmetic operators are: Plus (+), Minus (-), Multiplication (*), Division (/) and Modulus (%).

The **Plus** sign simply adds operands like **A + B**; where the value of the **B** adds to the value of the **A**.

The **Minus** sign acts on subtraction like **A – B**; where the value of the **B** subtracts from the value of the **A**.

The **Multiplication** sign multiplies operands like **A * B**; where the value of the **B** multiplies by the value of the **A**.

The **Division** sign performs division like **A / B;** where the value of the **A** divides by the value of the **B**.

We use these types of operators within mathematical formulae that are mostly used along with *assignment* operators.

Mathematical Operator		
Operator	Name	Example
+	Addition	A = B + C
-	Subtraction	A = B - C
*	Multiplication	A = B * C
/	Division	A = B / C
%	Modulus	A = B % C
++	Increment	A = B + +
--	Decrement	A = B --

Assignment operators

An assignment operator assigns a new value to the left side of operand. The assignment operator has this sign: "=". For example A = B + C; which adds the value of **C** to the **B** and simply assigns it to the **A**. If B =10 and C=15 then A=B+C, will assign 25 to the A.

Note: Do not get confused between simple assignment and the equal sign. Remember the equal has double signs such like "==", but an assignment has only one sign "=".

= *this is an assignment operator*

== *this is an equality operator*

In this formula A=B+C; you see the value C added to the B, and then the result of the addition is assigned to the A.

B and C are called operands and the A is called the operator.

Suppose a=5 and b=10 then consider **C =a = b ;** what will be the C-value?

Consider from right to the left. First the *b* which is 10 will be copied to the left which is the *a*, now the *a* becomes 10(value of *b* copied to the *a*). Now the value of the *a* will be copied to the *C*. So the *C* becomes 10.

If an expression is long you can use parentheses; parentheses are mostly used for clarity.

Another assignment operator is called the **Compound Operator**
For example you may want to increase a salary by 20 percent, then you can write:
Salary = Salary * 1.2;
Now the Salary at the right hand of the formula is increased by 20% and assigns its value to the left-hand salary. The second time you use Salary the value will be a new value.
Suppose your salary is $1000 and you want to increase it by 20%. Then you will write a compound statement **salary**=salary * 1.20;
Therefore the salary will be increased by the amount of $200. The new salary becomes $1200.
JavaScript provides many compound operators, look at some of these operators.

Compound Operators or Assignment Operator		
Operator	Example	Equivalent
+=	Total + =100	Total =Tota l + 100
-+	Total - =100	Total =Tota l - 100
*=	Total * =100	Total =Tota l * 100
/=	Total / =100	Total =Tota l / 100
%=	Total % =100	Total =Tota l % 100

You may write the compound operator (incremental operator) to add 1 integer to the X as one of these forms:
X=X+1;
X+=1;
++X;
X++;
You will learn more about the application of compound operators in the control structures of looping systems.

Now look at a basic JavaScript program that that performs basic mathematical operators.

Example: 6.3
```
1. <!DOCTYPE HTML PUBLIC "-//W3C//DTD HTML 4.01 Transitional//EN"
   "http://www.w3.org/TR/html4/loose.dtd">
2. <html>
3. <head>
4. <title>Basic Data</title>
5. <meta http-equiv="Content-Type" content="text/html; charset=iso-8859-1">
6. </head>
7. <body>
8. <script language="JavaScript" type="text/javascript">
9. var num1=10;
10.var num2=100;
11.var result;
12.document.write('<br> Addition:' + (num1+ num2));
13.document.write('<br> Division:' + (num1 / num2));
```

14. document.write('
 Subtraction:' +(num1-num2));
15. document.write('
 Modulus:' + (num2% num1));
16. </script>
17. </body>
18. </html>

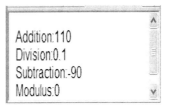

Addition:110
Division:0.1
Subtraction:-90
Modulus:0

The modulus or mode [%] operator calculates the remainder of a number. For example if you divide 10 / 3 the remainder will be 1.

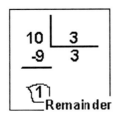

Relational operators

Relational operators are used to check and compare (comparison operator) two operands. They test the relationship between two operands and check if two operands are equal, or if one is greater than or less than the other. We use them mostly in conditional structures such as if-statements.

Relational operators have these signs: greater than (>), less than (<), and so on. Look at this table.

Relational Operators			
Name	**Symbol**	**Example**	**Status**
Greater than	>	2 > 3	False
Less than	<	2 < 3	True
Equal to	==	2 == 3	False
Greater than or equal	>=	2 >= 3	False
Less than or equal	<=	2 <= 3	True
Not equal	!=	2 != 3	True

Logical operators

Logical operators evaluate and combine two sides of operands. Logical operators are (**OR, AND, NOT**). The symbol for "AND" is **&&**; the symbol for "OR" is ||; and the symbol for "NOT" is "**!**".

Note: in **&&** (The **AND** Short circuit), two sides of the operand must be true. If one side is false, it does not check another side. In || (The **OR** Short circuit), at least one side must be true. If one side is true, it does not check the other side.

The bitwise (| and **&**) are acting differently which always checking two side of operand. They both act as binary, except the "NOT", which acts as unary.

Note: You will learn more about applications of these operators (*Arithmetic, Relational* and *Logical* operators) on the if-statements.

Type	Symbol	Example
AND	&&	((2<3)&&(4>5)) false, two sides must be true
OR	||	((2<3)||(4>5)) true, one sides must be true
NOT	!	If(!A>100)

Review questions
1- The use of **var** uses an option in JavaScript.   True   False
2- You can declare "Hello JavaScript" without using **var**.   True   False
3-The variable name must not be longer than 10 characters.   True   False
4- which of these declarations is (are) correct?
a. Y=100;
b. X=Hello Man;
c. **var** = hi;
d. **var** money=125.99;

5- What is the null declaration?
6- What is the output of document.write("this\\that")?
7- Correct document.write("I 'm wrong");
8- How does a new-line work in an alert box?
9- Which of these declarations is not correct?
a. **var** my name;
b. **var** 7pairs;
c. **var** numbers;

10- What is the difference between "=" and "=="?

Answer
1.   True
2.   True
3.   False
4.   A and D
5.   Declared but not initializing
6.   This\that
7.   'I \'m wrong'
8.   \r
9.   A and B
10. The first sign is an assignment operator and the second sign (==) is an equal sign

Chapter 7

Control Structures

- Introduction
- If-statement
- Multiple if-statements
- If-else statements
- Rule of braces
- Else-if/else-if

- Ternary operators
- If-statements Problems
- Using logical operator
- Prompt box
- Review questions
- Answers

Introduction

This chapter deals with the most fundamental programming structures. We try to explain these features as simply as possible. Computer programming language is structured the same as human languages. In daily speaking we might use many conditional statements such as "if you study hard or if you work hard" and so on. In computer language we also use the if-statement, if-else statement, ternary operator or switch statement. In fact the if-statement is used very frequently during programming procedures. We use operators along with conditional statements. The switch statement is an alternative for the if/else statement. In this chapter we try to present the ternary operator which acts the same as the if-statement.

If-statement

One of the most useful control structures is the *conditional statement*. The if-statement evaluates a condition; if the condition is true it will execute the related statement. You may have several if-statements, and the interpreter checks them one by one and evaluates them until it gets the true condition.

```
if (Boolean-expression)
{
Statement;
}
```

Look at this statement:
```
if(X>10)
{
document.write ("X is greater than 10");
}
```

So far there are two important things that you must always keep in your mind.
   1- if (Boolean-condition) should *not* be ended by a semi-colon.
   2- The expression must be *Boolean* type.

Let's look now at a simple example of an if-statement.

Example: 7.1
1. <!DOCTYPE HTML PUBLIC "-//W3C//DTD HTML 4.01 Transitional//EN"
    "http://www.w3.org/TR/html4/loose.dtd">
2. <html>
3. <head>
4. <title> If Statement </title>
5. <meta http-equiv="Content-Type" content="text/html; charset=iso-8859-1">
6. </head>
7. <body>
8. <script language="JavaScript" type="text/javascript">
9. <!--
10. var num1=10;
11. if(num1==10) {
12. document.write("Number 1 is = "+ num1);
13. }
14. -->
15. </script>
16. </body>
17. </html>

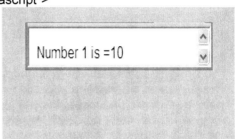

In the diagram below you see if the condition is true the program code will be executed, otherwise it goes nowhere.

The if-statement diagram

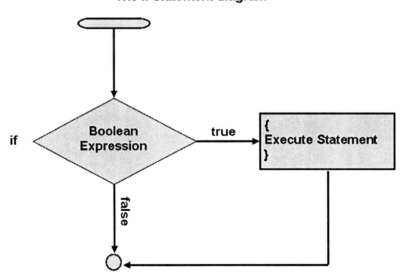

Multiple if-statements

There is no limit to using if-statements; you can use if-statements as many times as you want within a program. The program checks all if-statements one by one from top to bottom until it finds the true condition. Only the true condition will be executed. If the first condition is true then the program executes that statement and disregards the rest.

Look at this program; it identifies if a number is greater than, less than or equal to zero.

Example: 7.2

```
1.  <!DOCTYPE HTML PUBLIC "-//W3C//DTD HTML 4.01 Transitional//EN"
    "http://www.w3.org/TR/html4/loose.dtd">
2.  <html>
3.  <head>
4.  <title>Basic Data</title>
5.  <meta http-equiv="Content-Type" content="text/html; charset=iso-8859-1">
6.  </head>
7.  <body>
8.  <script language="JavaScript" type="text/javascript">
9.  <!--
10. var num1=10;
11. if(num1>10)
12. {
13. document.write("Number is greater than "+num1);
14. }
15. if(num1<10)
16. {
17. document.write("Number is less than "+num1);
18. }
19. if(num1==10)
20. {
21. document.write("Number is equal to "+num1);
22. }
23. -->
24. </script>
25. <br> You see the result of if-statement evaluation!
26. </body>
27. </html>
```

Number is equal to 10
You see the result of if-statement evaluation!

You see the JavaScript evaluates all condition until it finds the correct condition. What happens if there is no true condition? Then you must use an if-else statement.

If-else statements

So far when the condition was false the program could not do anything, but from now on we modify the program to execute the false statement and output the related message. There is another form of manipulating the if-statement, which is called the if/else statement. If you write a program that only uses if (one or several ifs) you can't control the program perfectly. When you are using *if-else* statements you have full control over your program execution. For example:

if(Age<16 && Age >90)
{
document.write*(" The ticket is half price");*
}

What happens if the user enters a number between the ranges of "16 to 90"? You see there will be no response. You will later see many business and science applications that force you to use else statements. Using an else clause is an usually option; however sometimes there is no choice and you have to use it, and in fact in many cases it is more convenient to use the *else* clause.

The if-statement with an else clause must execute either statement-1 or statement-2. If the condition is true then it executes statement-1, otherwise it executes the second statement.

if(Age > 100)
document.write *("Stay at home);*
else
document.write *("Take a trip);*

The if/else statement diagram

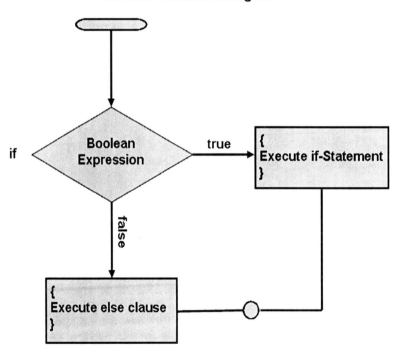

Example: 7.3

```
1.  <!DOCTYPE HTML PUBLIC "-//W3C//DTD HTML 4.01 Transitional//EN"
    "http://www.w3.org/TR/html4/loose.dtd">
2.  <html>
3.  <head>
4.  <title>if/elase statements</title>
5.  <meta http-equiv="Content-Type" content="text/html; charset=iso-8859-1">
6.  </head>
7.  <body>
8.  <script language="JavaScript" type="text/javascript">
9.  <!--
10. var str= "It checkes all conditions<br>";
11. var num1=10;
12. document.write(str);
13. if(num1>10)
14. {
15. document.write("Number is greater than
    "+ num1);
16. }
17. else
18. {
19. document.write("The else statement
    executed --> Number = "+num1);
20. }
21. -->
22. </script>
23. <br> You see the result of if-else
    statement evaluation!
24. </body>
25. </html>
```

It checkes all conditions
The else statement executed -->
Number= 10
You see the result of if-else
statement evaluation!

All conditions have been checked and there was no true statement found, therefore it executed the **else** clause.

Rule of braces

Braces, which are sometimes called *French braces*, are curly brackets "**{ }**" that are used to control statements. There must be an opened brace like this sign "**{**"and a closed brace like this sign"**}**". A block of statements must be placed inside the pair of braces.

```
if(Age>65)
{
document.write (" Time to retire! ");
document.write ("Time to travel!");
document.write ("Relax and study! ");
}
```

As you see, three statements are now placed between braces; they make up a **block** of statements. Why do we really need a block of statements? Is using the curly braces is an option or an obligation?

The answer is: if you have just one statement you do not need to place it inside the curly braces. However if you put a statement inside the braces it is still is valid, but remember if you have more than one statement then it is an obligation to use braces. In fact, braces make codes clean and readable. In JavaScript the brace may not be as important as it is in high level programming like Java.

Else-if/else-if

You can use else-if /else-if statements in a program several times

var Mark=75;
if (Mark >=90)
     document.write(" **A**");
 else if (Mark>=80)
    document.write (" **B**");
 else if(Mark>=70)
     document.write (" **C**");
else
    document.write (" **F**");

In the above case the result will be the letter C.
On the above code you see we used the relational operator.
Let's look at a program which outputs the result of the random numbers and check if the result is greater or less than the 6.

Example: 7.4

```
1.  <!DOCTYPE HTML PUBLIC "-//W3C//DTD HTML 4.01 Transitional//EN"
    "http://www.w3.org/TR/html4/loose.dtd">
2.  <html> <head>
3.  <title>if/elase statements</title>
4.  <meta http-equiv="Content-Type" content="text/html; charset=iso-8859-1">
5.  </head> <body>
6.  <script language="JavaScript" type="text/javascript">
7.  <!--
8.  var rand_no = Math.random();
9.  rand_no = rand_no * 10;
10. document.write(rand_no);
11. if(rand_no>6) {
12. document.write("<br>the number is greater than 6");
13. }
14. else {
15. document.write("<br>The number is less than 6");
16. document.write("<br>See the alert box"); }
17. alert(rand_no);
18. -->
19. </script> </body> </html>
```

2.3146216779440816
The number is less than 6
See the alret box

Windows Internet Explorer

!   2.3146216779440816

OK

The rand is multiplied by 10, so it limited the random generation between 1 to 10.
  rand_no = rand_no * 10;

Ternary operators

The ternary operator is an alternative to the *if-else* statements. Its syntax is very easy. The general form is:
(X>Y ? X : Y)
Read it as: if X>Y return to the X, otherwise return to the Y. The ternary operator reduces the source code, because the format is in one row, but if you are used to working with if-statements you may do so. If-else is even more flexible than the ternary operator.

Remark: The ternary operator must be ended with an else clause; if there is nothing to do then use the **null**, which is a keyword like:
(X>y)? X : null;

Example: 7.5
1. <!DOCTYPE HTML PUBLIC "-//W3C//DTD HTML 4.01 Transitional//EN" "http://www.w3.org/TR/html4/loose.dtd">
2. <html>
3. <head>
4. <title>if/elase statements</title>
5. <meta http-equiv="Content-Type" content="text/html; charset=iso-8859-1">
6. </head>
7. <body>
8. <script language="JavaScript" type="text/javascript">
9. <!--
10. var str ="Ternary operator checks conditions\r --------------------------";
11. var b=5;
12. (b == 5) ? Y="true" : Y="false";
13. alert(str+" \rThe result is:\t "+Y);
14. -->
15. </script>
16. </body>
17. </html>

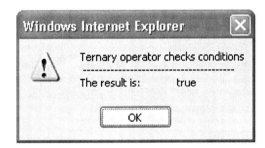

If-statements problems

Why we use the Ternary Operator? The answer is there is nothing wrong with the if-statement. Only the if-statement makes the source code bigger and hard to read, so for the reason of readability we may use Ternary Operators. Ternary Operators are clean, short and more readable.

Using logical operator

The logical operator such as && (AND) checks both side of the operand and both sides must be truc, while in the || (or) at least one side must be true.

Example: 7.6
1. <!DOCTYPE HTML PUBLIC "-//W3C//DTD HTML 4.01 Transitional//EN"
   "http://www.w3.org/TR/html4/loose.dtd">
2. <html>
3. <head>
4. <title> Logical Operator with if-statement </title>
5. <meta http-equiv="Content-Type" content="text/html; charset=iso-8859-1">
6. </head>
7. <body>
8. <script language="JavaScript" type="text/javascript">
9. <!--
10. var Salary = 75000;
11. if (Salary > = 50000 **&&** Salary < 95000)
12. {
13. document.write (" Salary range is between
    75000 to 95000 ");
14. }
15. else {
16. document.write (" Salary range is NOT
    between 75000 to 95000 ");
17. }
18. -->
19. </script>
20. </body>
21. </html>

Salary range is between
75000 to 95000

Try to change 95000 to 70000 then you will see the statement is not true, so the else clause will be executed.

Prompt box
The *prompt()* format is similar to **alert()** or **confirm()** but it creates a text field and allows data to be entered. In modern web pages the prompt may be usable anymore. It generates "OK" and "Cancel" buttons along with a textbox. The format of prompt is: prompt("Message", "default");

Example: 7.7
1. <!DOCTYPE HTML PUBLIC "-//W3C//DTD HTML 4.01 Transitional//EN"
   "http://www.w3.org/TR/html4/loose.dtd">
2. <html>
3. <head>
4. <title>Logical Operator with if-statement</title>
5. <meta http-equiv="Content-Type" content="text/html; charset=iso-8859-1">
6. </head>
7. <body>
8. <script language="JavaScript" type="text/javascript">
9. <!--
10. var name = prompt("Input your name in textbox ", "Your name here");

11. alert("Your name is: " + name);
12. -->
13. </script>
14. </body>
15. </html>

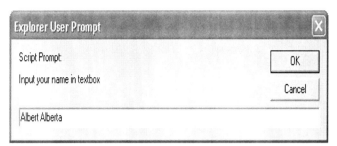 

The value of variable is string; the prompt knows only string and not numerical data.
Wait a minute! What happens if you want to enter integer or float numbers?
In case of numeral data we must return (convert) string to numeral data. JavaScript
provides two functions to convert string to numerical values. **parseInt()** and **parseFloat()**.
This example checks whether the number is odd or even.

Example: 7.8

1. <!DOCTYPE HTML PUBLIC "-//W3C//DTD HTML 4.01 Transitional//EN"
   "http://www.w3.org/TR/html4/loose.dtd">
2. <html> <head>
3. <title>Logical Operator with if-statement</title>
4. <meta http-equiv="Content-Type" content="text/html; charset=iso-8859-1">
5. </head> <body>
6. <script language="JavaScript" type="text/javascript">
7. <!--
8. var Num = prompt("Enter a number",
   "Input a number here!");
9. Num = parseInt(Num);
10. if (Num == 0) {
11. alert("You entered zero!");
12. }
13. else if (Num%2==0) {
14. alert(Num +" is an even number!");
15. }
16. else {
17. alert(Num +" is an odd number!");
18. }
19. -->
20. </script>
21. </body>
22. </html>

If you leave the box empty and press ok it generates a **NaN**(Not a Number).

The **switch** statement is a control statement that allows users to select an option from multiple selections, by pressing the related **case** option. In fact the switch statement is an alternative for the **if/else** statement. It is more convenient to use this when you have code that needs to choose from many options. The general format of a switch statement is as follows:

```
switch (expression)
            {
     case value-1 :
       statements-1
       break;
     case value-2 :
       statements-2
       break;
        .
        .
        .
     case value-n :
       statements-n
       break;
     default :
       statements
   } // end of switch statement
```

The switch statement must start with a switch keyword and a bracket which contains a defined variable. The **default** statement will be executed if no key match found.

Example: 7.9
1. <!DOCTYPE HTML PUBLIC "-//W3C//DTD HTML 4.01 Transitional//EN" "http://www.w3.org/TR/html4/loose.dtd">
2. <html>
3. <head>
4. <title>Switch Statement</title>
5. <meta http-equiv="Content-Type" content="text/html; charset=iso-8859-1">
6. </head> <body>
7. <script language="JavaScript" type="text/javascript">
8. <!--
9. var num=2;
10. switch(num) {
11. case 1:   {
12. document.write("
Did you press 1"); }
13. case 2:   {
14. document.write("
Did you press 2");
15. }

Did you press 2
Did you press 3
You must press 1,2 or 3

```
16. case 3:
17. {
18. document.write("<br>Did you press 3");
19. }
20. default:    {
21. document.write("<br>You must press 1,2 or 3");
22. }
23. } // end switch
24. -->
25. </script>
26. </body>
27. </html>
```

This program is not performing correctly. It must respond on a case not all cases. It must outputs "Did you press 2", Because the variable is set to 2. **So why?** Simple, because we did not use the **break** statement.

The corrected version will be like this:

Example: 7.10

```
1.  <!DOCTYPE HTML PUBLIC "-//W3C//DTD HTML 4.01 Transitional//EN"
    "http://www.w3.org/TR/html4/loose.dtd">
2.  <html>
3.  <head>
4.  <title>Switch statement</title>
5.  <meta http-equiv="Content-Type" content="text/html; charset=iso-8859-1">
6.  </head>
7.  <body>
8.  <script language="JavaScript" type="text/javascript">
9.  <!--
10. var num=2;
11. switch(num)
12. {
13. case 1: {
14. document.write("Did you press 1");
15. break; }
16. case 2: {
17. document.write("<br>Did you press 2");
18. break; }
19. case 3: {
20. document.write("<br>Did you press 3");
21. break; }
22. default: {
23. document.write("<br>You must press 1,2 or 3");
24. }
25. }
26. -->
27. </script> </body>
28. </html>
```

You can use a word like:
case "water" :
statement
case "food"
statement

Or you can use a letter like 'A' or 'b' uppercase or lowercase.

Laboratory exercise

A coffee shop is selling only three different sizes of coffees with different prices. The price of a small cup is $1.25, the price of a medium cup is $1.50, and the price of a large cup is $1.75. Suppose there are no taxes.

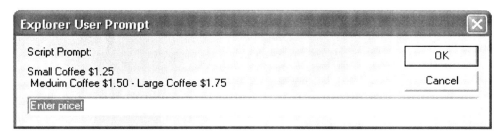

1. <!DOCTYPE HTML PUBLIC "-//W3C//DTD HTML 4.01 Transitional//EN" "http://www.w3.org/TR/html4/loose.dtd">
2. <html>
3. <head>
4. <title>Switch Statement</title>
5. <meta http-equiv="Content-Type" content="text/html; charset=iso-8859-1">
6. </head>
7. <body>
8. <script language="JavaScript" type="text/javascript">
9. <!--
10. var cafe;
11. cafe = prompt("Small Coffee $1.25\r Medium Coffee $1.50 - Large Coffee $1.75", "Enter price!");
12. switch ((cafe).toLowerCase())
13. {
14. case "large":
15. alert(cafe+" size Pay $1.75");
16. break;
17. case "medium":
18. alert(cafe+" size Pay $1.50");
19. break;
20. case "small":
21. alert(cafe+" size Pay $1.25");
22. break;

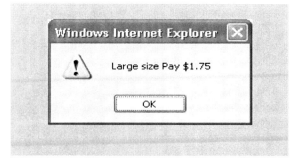

23. default:
24. alert("you must enter the coffee size");
25. }
26. -->
27. </script>
28. </body>
29. </html>

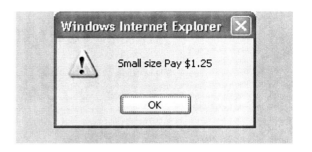

Chapter 8

Introduction

In this chapter we will discuss the second part of control structures. In the previous chapter we learned about if, if/else, ternary operators and switches. The chapter covered the importance of the if-statements. Here we continue the selection statements with the **Jump statements** such as (*break, continue, return, throw*). However, most of this chapter will be allocated to repetition statements, sometimes called looping statements, like (the *for,* the *while,* the *do-while*). Each of these statements is responsible for controlling the execution and behavior of the program. Using loops allows the programmer to repeat the execution procedures until the user terminates the program. It is rare to see a program with no looping system. The for loop, while loop and the do-while loops act the same way as the Java language. In the most efficient program we use combinations of the conditional statements (ifs or ternary and switches) with looping statements and jump statements.

Control Program

To control our code we use loops. The loop gives you the opportunity to have control over your program code, when should exit or repeat the execution of the code. As we have seen in if/else and switch statements, how we control a program to execute the true arguments, in the loop we control our code to repeat executions until the desirable points. JavaScript provides several loop systems namely the for-loop, the while-loop and the do-while loop. However we can modify them in different formats.

» The **for** loop
» The **while** loop
» The **do-while** loop

The for loop

The for loop repeats the execution until a specified condition evaluates to false. The JavaScript for loop is similar to the high level languages like Java and C++. The syntax is as follows:

```
for ([initial-expression;] [condition;] [increment-expression])
{
  Statements;
}
```

The *for* loop is used when we know how many times we want our loop to be performed. The **for** is a *keyword* and therefore can not be used as a variable.

Attention: Do not put a semi-colon at the end of the loop after the parentheses.
If you closely look at the general format of the for loop you see there are three parts.

» Initial part
» Conditional part
» Updating part, where updating means increment or decrement.

As program executes the initial expression is executes, it look at the condition the condition part is true the update the loop.
Look at a simple for loop that prints out 10 numbers from zero to nine.

Example: 8.1
1. <!DOCTYPE HTML PUBLIC "-//W3C//DTD HTML 4.01 Transitional//EN"
   "http://www.w3.org/TR/html4/loose.dtd">
2. <html>
3. <head>
4. <title>The for Loop Statement</title>
5. <meta http-equiv="Content-Type" content="text/html; charset=iso-8859-1">
6. </head>
7. <body>
8. <script language="JavaScript" type="text/javascript">
9. <!--
10. var number, Msg="";
11. for(number=0; number<10; number++)
12. {
13. Msg +=number+"\n";
14. }
15. alert(Msg);
16. -->
17. </script>
18. </body>
19. </html>

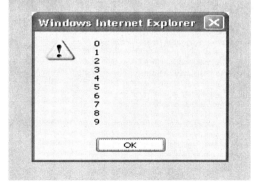

The compound operator Msg+=number is the same as Msg = Msg + number. It accumulates the result of a loop execution and stores it into the Msg(sting) the we use alert to print out the result. **Watch** the alert box is placed outside of the for loop.

Note: you can declare the **var** inside the for loop like this:
```
var  Msg="";
for(var number=0; number<10; number++)
{
Msg +=number+"\n";
}
alert(Msg);
```

You may want to declare the result of a loop and display it horizontally on the screen – in this case remove the \n (new-line).
Msg +=number+" ";

Exercise

Suppose you want to design a website that calculates and convert the degree of Celsius to Fahrenheit. It converts 10 to 20 Celsius to Fahrenheit and displays the result.

```
1.   <!DOCTYPE HTML PUBLIC "-//W3C//DTD HTML 4.01 Transitional//EN"
     "http://www.w3.org/TR/html4/loose.dtd">
2.   <html>
3.   <head>
4.   <title> Conversion </title>
5.   <meta http-equiv="Content-Type" content="text/html; charset=iso-8859-1">
6.   </head>
7.   <body>
8.   <script language="JavaScript" type="text/javascript">
9.   <!--
10. var  Msg="";
11. Line="Celsius    Fahrenheit\n--------\n";
12. var Cel, Fah;
13. for(var Cel=10; Cel<=20; Cel++)
14. {
15. Fah=1.8*Cel+32;
16. Msg = Msg+Cel+"         "+Fah+"\n";
17. }
18. alert(Line + Msg);
19. -->
20. </script>
21. </body>
22. </html>
```

Control digits

In the above example you see the decimal places have not been controlled, therefore it outputs unnecessary digits, as in: 55.400000000000006.

In JavaScript Number format will be done by using **toFixed()** method. The toFixed method takes any integer number. For example if you want to control the decimal places to two digits then it will be toFixed(2), as for three digits it will be toFixed(3).

Method	Description	Example
toFixed (x)	Formats any number of "x". The number is rounded up.	**Number.toFixed(2)** *Outputs two digits*
toPrecision(x)	Formats any number of "x" length. Which is called significant digits	**Number.toPrecision(x)**

Example: 8.2

```
1.  <!DOCTYPE HTML PUBLIC "-//W3C//DTD HTML 4.01 Transitional//EN"
    "http://www.w3.org/TR/html4/loose.dtd">
2.  <html>
3.  <head>
4.  <title>Control Decimal Points</title>
5.  <meta http-equiv="Content-Type" content="text/html; charset=iso-8859-1">
6.  </head>
7.  <body>
8.  <script language="JavaScript" type="text/javascript">
9.  <!--
10. var x, output="";
11. var Title="Digit        Result\n--------\n";
12. var num=9.3265418798;
13. for(x=1; x<10; x++)
14. {
15. output=output+x+"   "+ (num.toFixed(x)) +"\n";
16. }
17. alert(Title+output);
18. -->
19. </script>
20. </body>
21. </html>
```

If you change **toFixed(x)** with **toPercision(x)** then it generates this significant digits control.
To see it in the simple code. Use this code.
var num = 5.26541879;
document.write("With toFixed(2) ===

"+num.toFixed(2));
document.write("
 With toPrecision(2) =
"+num.toPrecision(2));
The above code produces this output:

With toFixed(2) === 9.33
With toPrecision(2)= 9.3

The while loop

The while loop executes the Boolean expression until the condition is true; when the condition becomes false, it stops executing. The syntax of the while loop is:

while(Boolean-Expression)
{
//Body of the program expected to be looped.
}
The while statement begins with the keyword **while**.

The *while* loop is checking the condition from beginning

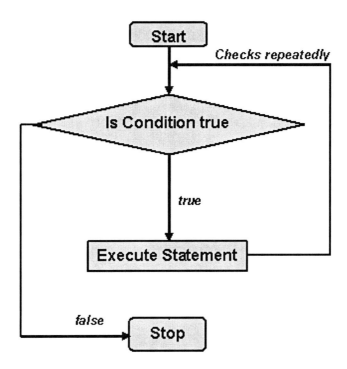

First you must declare the *initial value*, which the loop must start from, then set the Boolean *condition clause* and finally the value of the increment or the decrement (*Performance value*). As we mentioned above that the **for** loop contains 3 parts (initial part, conditional part and performance part), the same is correct for the **while** loop. For example:

int Values=1;   *// The initial value*
while(Values<=10) // **the conditional clause**
{
Values++; // *incremental performance*
}
Let's look at an example to see how the while loop works.

Example: 8.3
1. <!DOCTYPE HTML PUBLIC "-//W3C//DTD HTML 4.01 Transitional//EN"
    "http://www.w3.org/TR/html4/loose.dtd">
2. <html>
3. <head>
4. <title>The while loop</title>
5. <meta http-equiv="Content-Type" content="text/html; charset=iso-8859-1">

6. </head>
7. <body>
8. <script language="JavaScript" type="text/javascript">
9. <!--
10. var x=5;
11. var output="";
12. var title="The Result of Loops\n";
13. while(x<10)
14. {
15. output +=x+"\n";
16. x++;
17. }
18. alert(title+output);
19. -->
20. </script>
21. </body>
22. </html>

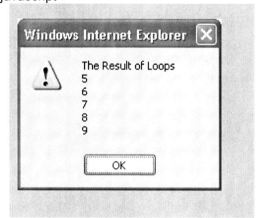

The X++; is incremented by 1 until value is true means less than 10(x<10).
The compound statement that you already learned increments or decrements the value,
Like this:
cnt +=1 ;
cnt - =1 ;
cnt++ ;
cnt-- ;
All of the above are incrementing or decrementing value of *counter* by **1** integer.
Note: you can use the compound operator inside the while loop like this:
while(++cnt <= 5), and do not use a semi-colon at the end of the bracket.
You may want to control the loop to perform up to the desired number, for example from 1 to 10 or any other number.

Example: 8.4
1. <!DOCTYPE HTML PUBLIC "-//W3C//DTD HTML 4.01 Transitional//EN"
    "http://www.w3.org/TR/html4/loose.dtd">
2. <html>
3. <head>
4. <title>The while loop</title>
5. <meta http-equiv="Content-Type" content="text/html; charset=iso-8859-1">
6. </head>
7. <body>
8. <script language="JavaScript" type="text/javascript">

```
9.  <!--
10. var x;
11. var y=1;
12. var output ="";
13. x=prompt("How many loops you want
    to perform"," Enter number" );
14. var title="looping from 1 to "+x+"\n";
15. while (y<=x)
16. {
17. output=output +y+ "\n";
18. y++;
19. }
20. alert(title + output);
21. -->
22. </script>
23. </body>
24. </html>
```

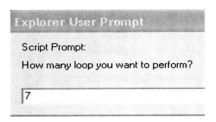

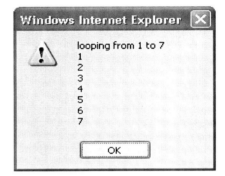

Jump statements

Jump statements cause a jump within a program. The most useful Jump statements are **break**, **continue**, and **return**.

Break

The break statement may be used to break out of a while, if, switch, do-while, or for statement. It simply stops (exits) a program loop. We already have seen the break statement within the switch statement.

```
var i=1;                            1
while (true) {                      2
if (i > 5)                          3
break;                              4
document.write("<br>"+i);          5
i++;
}
```

The above code prints numbers from 1 to 5, when numbers greater than 5 are reached then it automatically exits.

Continue

Continue statements force a program to execute according to the statement. The continue statement can be used to restart a loop. For example we can force a program to print out those numbers which are divisible by two.

```
output = "";
i=0;      //initial number
while (i < 10)    // conditional part
{
i++;      // incremental part
if (i>=4 && i<9) {
 continue;  }
 output += i+"<br>";
}
document.write(output);
```

1
2
3
9
10

Continue causes to get of loop according to the if-statement which is from 4 to 8. You see loop skip number 4 to 8 and can't print them.

Look at this code and answer the question, what number is not displayed onscreen?

```
var i=0
for (i=0;i<=5;i++)
{
if (i==3){continue}
document.write(i+" ")
}
```

Answer: number 3. The continue statement forces the loop to jump from number 3.

Using if-statements within a loop

We have already learned the if-statements and the switch statements in the previous chapter. In this chapter we try to put them together. The loop can be endless loop until we manage to stop it. We can change the behavior of the loop so it can act as we want it to. Here you see a loop with a condition. The **while (true)** means while the condition is true, which in this case it relays to your input.

If you want to calculate the total price, which is price + tax, then you use this formula: **Total = price * 1.07**. This is adding 7% tax to the price. We use a loop to repeat the procedures until we ask for an exit condition.

Example: 8.5
1. <!DOCTYPE HTML PUBLIC "-//W3C//DTD HTML 4.01 Transitional//EN"
    "http://www.w3.org/TR/html4/loose.dtd">
2. <html>
3. <head>
4. <title>Conditional while loop </title>
5. <meta http-equiv="Content-Type" content="text/html; charset=iso-8859-1">
6. </head>
7.   <body>
8. <script language="JavaScript" type="text/javascript">
9. <!--
10. var price;
11. var total;
12. while (true)

```
13. {
14. price=prompt("Enter price:\r Enter a
    negative number to exit:", "Price Here!");
15. if(price < 0)
16. break;
17. else
18. total= price * 1.07;
19. document.write("<br>Price => "+price+
    " Total => "+total);
20. }
21. -->
22. </script>
23. </body>
24. </html>
```

Explorer User Prompt

Script Prompt:

Enter price:
Enter a negative number to exit:

-9

Price => 100 Total => 107
Price => 200 Total => 214
Price => 300 Total => 321
Price => 500 Total => 535
Price => Price Here! Total => NaN

We entered 100, 200, 300 and 500. Enter a negative number to exit. It generates *NaN* (Not a Number) if you enter characters, and if you leave the box void then it outputs 0.

Do-while loop
The *do-while* loop acts exactly the same as the while loop except that the condition will be evaluated after the execution of the body of the program. Even if the initial condition is not true, still the do-while loop runs at least once. So the program executes at least once no matter whether the condition is true or false.

Syntax of do-while:
do
{
//statements
} while(Boolean-condition);

As you see, the statement is placed before the testing condition; therefore whether the initial condition is evaluated as true or false it will execute at least once. It executes once, then it checks if the condition is true or false.

The difference between the *do-while* loop and the *while* loop is that the while loop checks the condition at the beginning of the program and if the condition is true it will execute, otherwise it will exit. The do-while loop does not check the condition on the top, therefore it executes the loop anyway at least once.

The while sometimes is called *pre test* or *while-do*.

The do-while sometimes is called *post-test* or *do-while*.

The while loop	The do while loop
while(n >10) *{* *Loop body* *}*	*do* *{* *Loop body* *} while(n > 10);*

The Do-while loop executes at least once!

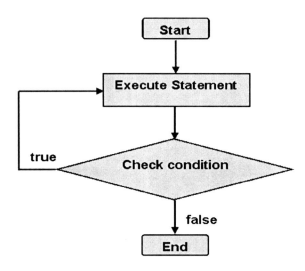

A simple do-while loop can be like this statement, which outputs from 0 to less than 10 and increases the value by 2.

```
var x = 0; // initial part
do
{
document.write("<br>Number: "+x);
x+=2;  //incremental part
}
while(x<10);  // conditional part
```

```
Number: 0
Number: 2
Number: 4
Number: 6
Number: 8
```

We try to write a program that prints out the area of a circle; while its radius is between 10 to 20, it calculates all even numbers, for example radius of 10, 12, 14 and … then it prints out the area.

Example: 8.6

```
1. <!DOCTYPE HTML PUBLIC "-//W3C//DTD HTML 4.01 Transitional//EN"
   "http://www.w3.org/TR/html4/loose.dtd">
2. <html>
3. <head>
4. <title> do... while loop </title>
5. <meta http-equiv="Content-Type" content="text/html; charset=iso-8859-1">
6. </head>
7. <body>
8. <script language="JavaScript" type="text/javascript">
9. <!--
10. var radius = 10;
11. var area;
12. var output=" ";
13. var title="Radius      Area\n";
14. do
15. {
16. area=Math.PI*radius*radius;
17. radius+=2;
18. area=area.toFixed(2);
19. output=output+ radius+"    "+area +"\n";
20. }
21. while(radius<20);
22. alert(title + output);
23. -->
24. </script>
25. </body>
26. </html>
```

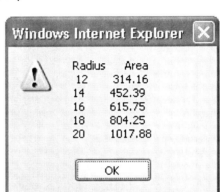

We use **Math.PI**, the PI is known to the interpreter of JavaScript, therefore you do not need to declare PI = 3.14...xxxxxxxxx. We will learn more about Math library in the next chapter.

Loops comparison

The three types of loops actually act the exact same way. We use them for different purposes. For example we use the while loop when we want the program to check the condition from the beginning. We use the for loop when we know how may time the loop is performing and finally with use the do-while loop when we want a program to execute at least once.

Loops comparison		
The for loop	**The while loop**	**The do-while loop**

var x;
for(x=0; x<5; x++) {
document.write("
Numb
er: "+x); }
All written on one line.
x = 0; //initial
x< 5; //condition
x++ // increment
	var x = 0; // initial
	while(x<5) //condition
	{
	document.write("
	Numb
	er: "+x);
	x+=1; // increment
	}
		var x = 0; //initial
		do
		{
		document.write("
		Numb
		er: "+x);
		x+=1; //increment
		} while(x<5); //condition

Number: 0 Number: 1 Number: 2 Number: 3 Number: 4	Number: 0 Number: 1 Number: 2 Number: 3 Number: 4	Number: 0 Number: 1 Number: 2 Number: 3 Number: 4

Review questions
1. Give a short description of the while loop.
2. Give a short description of the do-while loop.
3. Give a short description of the for loop.
4. What are the three important parts of a loop?
5. What is the X+=2;
6. var total= 99.9958; how do you control the total to two digits?
7. What is the break statement?
8. What is the continue statement?
9. The while (true) loop runs 10 times.   True   False
10. The Math.PI is understood by the JavaScript interpreter. True   False

Answer
1. The while loop checks conditions from the beginning and if a condition is false then it stops the execution.
2. The do-while executes a loop at least once, regardless of condition.
3. The for loop repeats the execution until a specified condition evaluates to false, we use it when we know how may times we want to perform it.
4. Initial, conditional, incremental.
5. Each time, adds 2 to the x-value
6. total.toFixed(2);
7. exits the program
8. Skips from some execution according to the condition.
9. False, it generates an endless loop.
10. True.

Chapter 9

Introduction

In JavaScript functions are sets of codes that perform special tasks. In fact there are many predefined functions in JavaScript. In JavaScript you might use two types of functions. One is called a predefined function, such as those which exist in the JavaScript interpreter. For example: alert(), prompt(), confirm() or the static methods of the math library like(*sqrt, floor, abs*) and so on. The second type of function is called a User Defined function, where you define your own function (create a function). There is almost no program that is written without using the power of functions. In fact functions give great visibility to the program, simply because it divides the program into several parts, that's why they are sometimes called subprograms. In this chapter we try to learn built-in and predefined functions in an easy way.

Built-in function

In JavaScript there are several ways to create functions. What is the built-in function? The built-in functions are those functions that exist inside the JavaScript library and we just call such function to perform their tasks. We have already seen some of these functions like **alert()**, prompt(), write() and rand(). Let look at the confirm box.

Confirm boxes

A JavaScript confirmation box gives your visitors a choice of whether they want to confirm or cancel an action. It is a pop up like an alert box, but provides two buttons, "OK" and "Cancel". The simple format of a confirm box is:

confirm("Do you really want to confirm it?");

Remember if you use the above format, it isn't very useful. You must take advantages of true or false values that the confirmation box provides for you. In order to use the confirmation box in an efficient way, you may assign it to some variable like:
var DoIt= confirm("Do you really want to confirm it?");

The "DoIt" is a variable that allow us to use it for some operations, for example:
if (DoIt== true)
{
  //statements
}
else
{
Other statements
}
Look at this example:

Example: 9.1
1. <!DOCTYPE HTML PUBLIC "-//W3C//DTD HTML 4.01 Transitional//EN"
   "http://www.w3.org/TR/html4/loose.dtd">
2. <html>
3. <head>
4. <title>Confirm Boxes </title>
5. <meta http-equiv="Content-Type" content="text/html; charset=iso-8859-1">
6. </head>
7. <body>
8. <script language="JavaScript" type="text/javascript">
9. <!--
10. var currentTime = new Date()
11. var hours = currentTime.getHours()
12. var minutes = currentTime.getMinutes()
13. var answer = confirm ("Do you want to see
    time? \r Choose OK or Cancel ")
14. if (answer == true)
15. alert("Now time is: "+hours + ":" + minutes)
16. else
17. alert("So, you don't like to see the time!");
18. -->
19. </script>
20. </body>
21. </html>

Instead of **if (answer==true)** you can use **if(answer)**.

Mathematical functions
Mathematical functions are built-in functions and you can use them by calling a function, for example an absolute number.
abs(number), like abs(-9.3); which returns to the absolute value of 9.3.
All values of trigonometric functions must be in radian and not in degree.
1 radian = **180/**π degrees, and 1 degree = π**/180** radians.

JavaScript provides these mathematical functions.

Math.abs(a)   // the absolute value
Math.cos(a)   // cosine
Math.acos(a)   // arc cosine
Math.sin(a)   // sine
Math.asin(a)   // arc sine
Math.atan(a)   // arc tangent
Math.atan2(a,b) // arc tangent
Math.ceil(a)   // rounded to top
Math.floor(a)   // rounded down
Math.exp(a)   // exponent
Math.log(a)   // log of a base e
Math.max(a,b)   // the maximum
Math.min(a,b)   // the minimum
Math.pow(a,b)   // a to the power b
Math.random()   // random number in the range 0 to 1
Math.round(a)   // integer closest to a
Math.sin(a)   // sine
Math.sqrt(a)   // square root
Math.tan(a)   // tangent
Also a static method of PI() return the value of 3.1416...

Let's look at some mathematical built-in functions in JavaScript.

Example: 9.2

```
 1. <!DOCTYPE HTML PUBLIC "-//W3C//DTD HTML 4.01 Transitional//EN"
    "http://www.w3.org/TR/html4/loose.dtd">
 2. <html>
 3. <head>
 4. <title>Mathematical Functions </title>
 5. <meta http-equiv="Content-Type" content="text/html; charset=iso-8859-1">
 6. </head>
 7. <body>
 8. <script language="JavaScript" type="text/javascript">
 9. <!--
10. document.write("Absolute value is:
    "+Math.abs(-10.57));
11. document.write("<br>Cos 0 is:
    "+Math.cos(0));
12. document.write("<br>acos 0 is:
    "+Math.acos(0).toFixed(2));
13. document.write("<br>Sin 0 is:
    "+Math.sin(0));
14. document.write("<br>Ceil 4.23 is:
    "+Math.ceil(4.23));
15. document.write("<br>Floor 4.23 is:
    "+Math.cos(4.23) toFixed(2));
```

16. document.write("
Minimum 10 and 20 is: "+Math.min(10,20));
17. document.write("
Power 2 to 4 is: "+Math.pow(2,4));
18. document.write("
Random 0 to 1 is: "+Math.random().toFixed(2));
19. document.write("
Round 4.23 is: "+Math.round(4.23));
20. document.write("
Squeare root of 9 is: "+Math.sqrt(9));
21. document.write("
The PI value: "+Math.PI());
22. -->
23. </script>
24. </body>
25. </html>

Absolute value is: 10.57
Cos 0 is: 1
acos 0 is: 1.57
Sin 0 is: 0
Ceil 4.23 is: 5
Floor 4.23 is: -0.46
Minimum 10 and 20 is: 10
Power 2 to 4 is: 16
Random 0 to 1 is: 0.72
Round 4.23 is: 4
Squeare root of 9 is: 3

Date and time

There are some nice date, time and calendar which JavaScript provides for us. These functions (methods) exist inside the JavaScript interpreter. We try to look at some methods that we usually use in our websites.

» **getDate()**   Day of the month (0-31)
» **getTime()**   Number of milliseconds since 1/1/1970 at 12:00 AM
» **getSeconds()**   Number of seconds (0-59)
» **getMinutes()**   Number of minutes (0-59)
» **getHours()**   Number of hours (0-23)
» **getDay()**   Day of the week(0-6) where 0 = Sunday, ... and 6 = Saturday
» **getMonth()**   Number of month (0-11)
» **getFullYear()**   The four digit year (1970-9999)

The simple date and time that are provided by default is **Date( )**. If you just use it with document.write you will see the output.
document.write(Date());

Sun Feb 03 07:55:49 2008

Example: 9.3
1. <!DOCTYPE HTML PUBLIC "-//W3C//DTD HTML 4.01 Transitional//EN" "http://www.w3.org/TR/html4/loose.dtd">
2. <html>
3. <head>
4. <title>
5. Date and Tme
6. </title>
7. <meta http-equiv="Content-Type" content="text/html; charset=iso-8859-1">
8. </head>
9. <body>

```
10.<script language="JavaScript" type="text/javascript">
11.<!--
12.var d = new Date()
13.var day = d.getDate()
14.var month = d.getMonth() + 1
15.var year = d.getFullYear()
16.document.write("In The dd,mm,yyyy format<br>
    now is: "+day+ "/" + month  + "/" + year)
17.-->
18.</script>
19.</body>
20.</html>
```

In The dd,mm,yyyy format now is: 2/2/2008

Let modify the above program, so when a user visits your website then it messages out according to the local time. For example, if a user visits in the morning it says "Good Morning" or if it is the afternoon it display a message like "Good afternoon!".

Example: 9.4

```
1.  <!DOCTYPE HTML PUBLIC "-//W3C//DTD HTML 4.01 Transitional//EN"
    "http://www.w3.org/TR/html4/loose.dtd">
2.  <html> <head>
3.  <title>Hours </title>
4.  <meta http-equiv="Content-Type" content="text/html; charset=iso-8859-1">
5.  </head> <body>
6.  <script language="JavaScript" type="text/javascript">
7.  <!--
8.  var d = new Date()
9.  var day = d.getDate()
10. var month = d.getMonth() + 1
11. var year = d.getFullYear()
12. var hours = d.getHours()
13. var minutes = d.getMinutes()
14. if (minutes < 10)
15. minutes = "0" + minutes
16. document.write("Date and Time:
    "+day+":"+month+":"+year)
17. document.write("<br> Time is: "+hours+
    ":"+minutes)
18. if(hours>=5 && hours<12)
19. document.write("<br>Good Morning");
20. if(hours>12 && hours<=18)
21. document.write("<br>Good afternoon!");
22. if(hours>18 && hours<=24)
23. document.write("<br>Good Evening!");
24. -->
25. </script> </body> </html>
```

Date and Time: 2:2:2008
Time is: 17:07
Good afternoon!

We can also use the date and time to apply on our website. For example you want to visit **Google** and **Yahoo** on an alternating schedule, meaning on the even days you see Google and on the odd days you see yahoo.
window.location provides a facility to redirect your website to the selected path.

Example: 9.5

```
1.  <!DOCTYPE HTML PUBLIC "-//W3C//DTD HTML 4.01 Transitional//EN"
      "http://www.w3.org/TR/html4/loose.dtd">
2.  <html> <head>
3.  <title>Website Location </title>
4.  <meta http-equiv="Content-Type" content="text/html; charset=iso-8859-1">
5.  </head> <body>
6.  <script language="JavaScript" type="text/javascript">
7.  <!--
8.  var d = new Date()
9.  var day = d.getDate()
10. document.write("Today is: "+day);
11. if(day % 2==0)
12. window.location ="http://www.google.com/";
13. else
14. window.location ="http://www.yahoo.com/";
15. -->
16. </script> </body>
17. </html>
```

Digital clock

JavaScript provides several built-in functions that help to create a moveable or animated clock. Some methods are self-descriptive, such as:
getSeconds(); //to get seconds
getMinutes(); //to get minutes
getHours(); // to get hours
There are two methods that both act almost the same way.
setTimeout (expression, timeout); it runs until you stop the time out.
You can use **clearTimeout()** method to clear out the result of setTimeout.
setInterval (expression, interval); is almost the same as the setTimeout() method.
The **clearInterval()** method is used if you want to cancel a setInterval().

Example: 9.6

```
1.  <!DOCTYPE HTML PUBLIC "-//W3C//DTD HTML 4.01 Transitional//EN"
      "http://www.w3.org/TR/html4/loose.dtd">
2.  <html> <head>
3.  <title> Digital Clock </title>
4.  <meta http-equiv="Content-Type" content="text/html; charset=iso-8859-1">
5.  <script language="JavaScript" type="text/javascript">
6.  <!--
7.  var str;
```

```
8.  function digitalClock() {
9.  var now = new Date();
10. var seconds = now.getSeconds();
11. var minutes = now.getMinutes();
12. var hours = now.getHours();
13. str = hours;
14. str += ((minutes < 10) ? ":0" : ":") + minutes;
15. str += ((seconds < 10) ? ":0" : ":") + seconds;
16. str += (hours >= 12) ? " PM" : " AM";
17. document.digitalClock.clock.value = str;
18. setTimeout("digitalClock()", 1000); }
19. -->
20. </script>   </head>
21. <body onLoad="digitalClock()">
22. <form name="digitalClock">
23. Digital Clock:
24. <input type="text" name="clock"
       size="10" value="" ><br>
25. </form>   </body>
26. </html>
```

Digital Clock: 5:47:15 AM

You can change intervals to different numbers; here it is set to 1000 to convert milliseconds to seconds.

Here you see some useful date and time letters that JavaScript provides.

Letter	Description
d	Day of the month as one digits(single digit)
dd	Day of the month as two digits(leading zero)
ddd	Day in three-letter abbreviation
dddd	Day in full name
m	Month as a digits
mm	Month of the month as two digits(leading zero)
mmm	Month with three-letter abbreviation
mmmm	Month in full name
yy	Year as last two digits, leading zero
yyyy	Year as four digits.
h	Hours with no leading zero in a single-digit (12-hour clock)
hh	Hours with leading zero in a single-digit (12-hour clock)
H	Hours with no leading zero in a single-digit (24-hour clock)
HH	Hours with leading zero in a single-digit (24-hour clock)
M	Minutes with no leading zero in a single-digit
MM	Minutes with leading zero in a single-digit
s	Seconds with no leading zero in a single-digit
ss	Seconds with leading zero in a single-digit

The difference between two periods can be calculated as:
var d = new Date()
var born = new Date("8/25/1955")
var diff = Math.floor((d.getTime()
- born.getTime()) / 86400000) *//To remove millisecond 1000/60/60/24*
var msg = + diff + " days from "+born;
document.write(msg)

19155 days from Thu Aug 25 00:00:00 PDT 1955

User defined functions

In spite of the many methods or predefined functions that exist in JavaScript, still we need to have some options to customize our own function. For example, if you want to add two integer numbers you can create a function and call it **Add( )**. A function is sometimes called a subprogram, because a function is a set of program code that acts as a program. In JavaScript using a function sometimes is necessary; you will rarely see a JavaScript code without some functions, in fact functions are a central unit of JavaScript. Usually the User Defined Function has three major parts:

▶ Function Definition
▶ Function Call
▶ Function return

Function definition
The function definition consists of a function header and its body. The header must start with a **function** keyword then a function-Name. The syntax is similar to this:
function functionName
{
}
You see the function keyword and the name of the function followed by curly brackets. The body of a function is situated inside of the body.

function functionName
{
// body of function
}

Function call

The function call is nothing but calling the function name. For example if you create a function like:
function Test // function definition
{
alert("I am a function"); // function body that is inside bracket
}
Test(); // this is function call

Basic function

In fact, the basic function can be built by using a definition and calling part without the complication of the other parts.

Example: 9.7

```
1.  <!DOCTYPE HTML PUBLIC "-//W3C//DTD HTML 4.01 Transitional//EN"
     "http://www.w3.org/TR/html4/loose.dtd">
2.  <html>
3.  <head>
4.  <title>Simple Function </title>
5.  <meta http-equiv="Content-Type" content="text/html; charset=iso-8859-1">
6.  </head>
7.  <body>
8.  <script language="JavaScript" type="text/javascript">
9.  <!--
10. function Dog() //function definition
11. {
12. document.write('Dog is a nice animal!');
        //body
13. }
14. Dog();  //calling function
15. //-->
16. </script>
17. </body>
18. </html>
```

Dog is a nice animal!

Unlike many programming languages, JavaScript functions do not need to be defined before calling. You can call the function then define it.

```
Dog(); // call function
  function Dog()
  {
  document.write('Dog is a nice animal!');
  }
```

Sometimes you want a button that works automatically upon the touch of the mouse. You can use a function and use onMouseOver to work and display a message as you want.

Example: 9.8

```
1.  <!DOCTYPE HTML PUBLIC "-//W3C//DTD HTML 4.01 Transitional//EN"
     "http://www.w3.org/TR/html4/loose.dtd">
2.  <html>
3.  <head>
4.  <title> Function with Parameter </title>
5.  <meta http-equiv="Content-Type" content="text/html; charset=iso-8859-1">
6.  <script language="JavaScript" type="text/javascript">
```

```
7.  <!--
8.  function AutoDispaly()
9.  {
10. alert("Touch button without click! ");
11. }
12. //-->
13. </script>
14. </head>
15. <body>
16. <input type="button" value="Just Touch Me!"
        onMouseOver="AutoDispaly();">
17. </body>
18. </html>
```

Function with parameters

Sometimes you want to use parameters with a function.

function Msg() // this is without parameter.

Function Msg(text) this function has the parameter "text". The Msg is just the function name.

The parameter is sometimes called the argument.

Example: 9.9

```
1.  <!DOCTYPE HTML PUBLIC "-//W3C//DTD HTML 4.01 Transitional//EN"
       "http://www.w3.org/TR/html4/loose.dtd">
2.  <html>
3.  <head>
4.  <title> Function with Parameter </title>
5.  <meta http-equiv="Content-Type" content="text/html; charset=iso-8859-1">
6.  </head>
7.  <body>
8.  <script language="JavaScript" type="text/javascript">
9.  <!--
10. function Msg(text) {
11. document.write(text);
12. }
13. Msg('Using function is easy');
14. Msg('<br>and funny!');
15. //-->
16. </script>
17. </body>
18. </html>
```

Using function is easy and funny!

Now what happens if you have two or three or even more things to do? We use multiple parameters.

Multiple parameters

You have seen the single parameter, so in the same way we can create multiple parameters. First try to look at this function.

```
<script language="JavaScript">
function Msg1(){alert("I am from Msg1 function!");}
function Msg2(){alert("I am from Msg2 function!");}
</script>
</head>
<body>
<input type="button" value="See Msg1 Function" onMouseOver="Msg1() "><br>
<input type="button" value="See Msg2 Function" onMouseOver="Msg2() ">
 </body>
```

The above function does not have any parameter, it's called void parameter.
The above code produces this result:

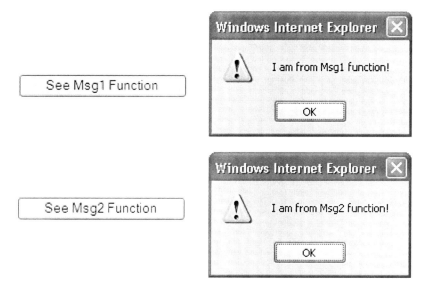

Now we can use parameters. The parameters are actually variables sitting inside parentheses in front of a function like:
 function MyFunction(a, b){ } // a and b both are parameters.

What we really do by using parameters. Let's ask what happens if you have many messages. Do you create many functions? The answer is NO. I do not create many functions and in fact I create only one function with different parameters and pass the values of parameters; but how? Let see:

Example: 9.10

```
1.  <!DOCTYPE HTML PUBLIC "-//W3C//DTD HTML 4.01 Transitional//EN"
    "http://www.w3.org/TR/html4/loose.dtd">
2.  <html>
3.  <head>
4.  <title> Function with Parameter </title>
5.  <meta http-equiv="Content-Type" content="text/html; charset=iso-8859-1">
6.  <script language="JavaScript" type="text/javascript">
7.  <!--
8.  function Volume(x, y, z)
9.  {
10. var output="";
11. var Vol = (x * y * z)
12. document.write ("Your volume is: " + Vol + " <br> ");
13. }
14. //-->
15. </script>
16. </head>
17. <body>
18. <script language="JavaScript" type="text/javascript">
19. <!--
20. Volume(2,3,4);
21. Volume(2,5,7);
22. Volume(7,8,9);
23. //-->
24. </script>
25. </body>
26. </html>
```

Your volume is: 24
Your volume is: 70
Your volume is: 504

Function with return

Each function must return to its value, here in JavaScript a function can simply return the value. For example: **return** ("I am returning from a function Msg!"); which returns the string message.

Example: 9.11

```
1.  <!DOCTYPE HTML PUBLIC "-//W3C//DTD HTML 4.01 Transitional//EN"
    "http://www.w3.org/TR/html4/loose.dtd">
2.  <html>
3.  <head>
4.  <title> Function with return </title>
5.  <meta http-equiv="Content-Type" content="text/html; charset=iso-8859-1">
```

```
6.  </head>
7.  <body>
8.  <script language="JavaScript" type="text/javascript">
9.  <!--
10. function Msg() {
11. return ("I am returning from a function Msg!");
12. }
13. document.write(Msg());
14. //-->
15. </script>  </body>
16. </html>
```

I am returning from a function Msg!

Here you see a function with return and parameters

```
function Add(a, b) //parameters
{
 return a+b; // return value
}
document.write(Add(10,15));  // call function
```

Putting functions into action

So far we have worked with functions but we have not entered values; the values were already set inside the code. Now we will try to work with functions more dynamically. For that purpose we create a form boxes which allows users to enter numbers. Look at the example.

We designed the form with CSS style. The function **addThem** has been created to add numbers.

Note: because every variable is treaded as string therefore we parse them to be floated.

document.add.Ans.value = parseFloat(document.add.num1.value)

add	→name of form
Ans	→name of the answer box, in this case Total
num1	→textbox for number 1
value	→ is known within the form
parseFloat	→ convert string to float number

Example: 9.12

```
1.  <!DOCTYPE HTML PUBLIC "-//W3C//DTD HTML 4.01 Transitional//EN"
     "http://www.w3.org/TR/html4/loose.dtd">
2.  <html>
3.  <head>
4.  <title> Digital Clock </title>
5.  <meta http-equiv="Content-Type" content="text/html; charset=iso-8859-1">
6.  <style type="text/css">
7.  <!--
```

```
8.  body{background-color: yellow;
9.  color: blue;
10. text-align: center;
11. border-style: solid dotted;
12. width: 200px;}
13. -->
14. </style>
15. <script language="JavaScript" type="text/javascript">
16. <!--
17. function addThem()
18. {
19. document.add.Ans.value = parseFloat(document.add.num1.value) +
    parseFloat(document.add.num2.value)
20. }
21. function clearform()
22. {
23. document.add.num1.value= " ";
24. document.add.num2.value= " ";
25. document.add.Ans.value= " ";
26. }
27. -->
28. </script>
29. </head>
30. <body>
31. <form  action="" name="add">
32. Number 1:
33. <input type="text" name="num1" size=8 maxlength="7"><br>
34. Number 2:
35. <input type="text" name="num2" size="8" maxlength="7"><br>
36. Total:
37. <input  type="text" name="Ans" size="5" maxlength="5"><br>
38. <input  type="button" value ="Add Them" name="Submit"   onClick="addThem()">
39. <input type="button" name="Submit2" value="Clear form" onClick="clearform()">
40. </form>
41. </body>
42. </html>
```

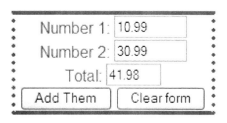

Review questions

1. What is a built-in function?
2. All mathematical functions producing output I degree   True   False
3. In order to work with PI you have to declare PI, because it does not exist in JavaScript.   True   False
4. What does the getDay() method produce?
5. To get the default full path, day and time you just use: document.write(Date());
                                                                True   False
6. What does the window.location command do in JavaScript?
7. Why do we usually use 1000 for intervals in the setTimeout method?
8. The function itself is a keyword.   True   False
9. A function can have many parameters like: function MyFunction(a, b, c){ }
                                                                True   False
10. If your form name is "add" and your textbox name is "num1" then this statement will clear the box. document.add.num1.value= " ";   True   False

Answer

1. A set of methods that may be used without creating them from scratch.
2. False
3. False
4. Day of the week(0-6) where 0 = Sunday, ... and 6 = Saturday
5. True
6. **window.location** provides a facility to redirect your website to the selected path.
    e.g. window.location ="http://www.google.com/";
7. To return millisecond to second
8. True
9. True
10. True

Chapter 10

Introduction

The array system is a basic concept of data structures, which makes the array system one of the most important topics to learn. In fact array allows us to store data quite easily. The data can be stored for later implementations. Array is an organized storage; the elements inside an array can be accessed by their indices. We use arrays to prevent the declaration of a large number of variables, which, interestingly, can be done by using a single array declaration. Because the data is nicely arranged in the array system according to their indices, which starts from 0 to the last index of element therefore the search for elements and sorting elements, become significantly easy. Arrays can be declared as single dimensional or multidimensional forms. JavaScript provides many easy methods which leads to shorter code and increases the efficiency levels. In this chapter we learn about string and application of string in JavaScript. In many situations we need to use string for the text implementation.

Basic arrays

An array object is used to collect a set of variables in a variable name. Instead of declaring a variable-name for each name, we just using one variable name and store all names inside the declared variable. For example if you have four names, in a regular variable's declaration you must declare and assign a variable for each name like:
var name1="Peter";
var name2="Bob";
var name3="Jack";
var name4="Isabelle";

Now instead of using name1, name2 and so on you just use one variable name.
var names=new Array("Peter", "Bob", "Jack", "Isabelle");
When elements are set in the array, each element has an index which starts from 0 to last element. In this case you see "Peter" has the index of zero while "Isabelle" has 3.

Because indexes start from zero, therefore the last index is last minus 1, meaning the forth element has the index of 3.

Note: The array is understood by the JavaScript interpreter and the **A** of Array has to be in uppercase letters like this: **A**rray.

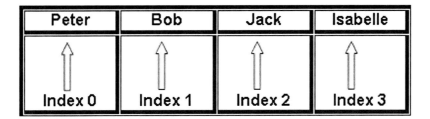

Array declaration

An array can be single or multidimensional (two or more dimensions), depending on how you declare them. A simple declaration like:

var names=new Array("Peter", "Bob", "Jack", "Isabelle");

You can declare the above array like this:

var name=new Array();
name[0]= **"Peter";**
name[1]= **"Bob";**
name[2]= **"Jack";**
name[3]= **"Isabelle";**

Example: 10.1

1. <!DOCTYPE HTML PUBLIC "-//W3C//DTD HTML 4.01 Transitional//EN"
   "http://www.w3.org/TR/html4/loose.dtd">
2. <html> <head>
3. <title> Simple Array </title>
4. <meta http-equiv="Content-Type" content="text/html; charset=iso-8859-1">
5. </head> <body>
6. <script language="JavaScript" type="text/javascript">
7. <!--
8. var output="";
9. output+="The contents of array:\r----------------\r";
10. var name=new Array("Peter ", " Bob", " Jack", " Isabelle");
11. output+=(name[0]+"\r"+name[1]+"\r"+name[2]+"\r"+name[3]);
12. alert(output);
13. -->
14. </script> </body>
16. </html>

You can call each array element separately, like:
var name=new Array()
name[0]= "Peter , ";
name[1]= "Bob , ";
name[2]= "Jack , ";
name[3]= "Isabelle ";
document.write(name[0],name[1],name[2],name[3]);

We can assign some names to our array later on, by using another array object like:
names[0]="Dog";
names[2]="Cat";
Check out this example, which is done in JavaScript and CSS code.

Example: 10.2

```
1. <!DOCTYPE HTML PUBLIC "-//W3C//DTD HTML 4.01 Transitional//EN"
   "http://www.w3.org/TR/html4/loose.dtd">
2. <html> <head>
3. <title> Call new Array </title>
4. <meta http-equiv="Content-Type" content="text/html; charset=iso-8859-1">
5. <style type="text/css">
        <!--
6. body{background-color: yellow;
7. color: blue;
8. text-align: center;
9. border-style:  dotted;
10. width: 250px;}
        -->
11. </style>
12. <script language="JavaScript" type="text/javascript">
        <!--
13. names=new Array("Peter", "Jack",
    "Susan", "Barbara");
14. document.write(names + "<br>" +
    names[2] + "<br>");
15. document.write("New names
    assigned to the array:<br>");
16. names=new Array();
17. names[0]="Dog";
18. names[2]="Cat";
19. document.write(names);
        -->
20. </script> </head>
21. <body>
22. </body>
23. </html>
```

Peter,Jack,Susan,Barbara
Susan
New names assigned to the array:
Dog,,Cat

Look at the output, between Dog and Cat there are two comas which is an indication of an empty array.

Array and loops

So far the advantage of array declaration was only putting several elements into one variable name. In fact, without using loops array systems become almost useless. Arrays and loops fell in love a long time ago and they are still together. The more useful loop is the *for* loop.

```
var number = new Array(40,60,70,100,90,65.5);
var sum = number[3]+number[5];
document.write("Sum of index 3 and index 5: "+sum);
```

* Sum of index 3 and index 5: 165.5 *

In the above example you see we chose numbers with 3 and 5 indexes and we add them up. Now what happens if you have many numbers, 10, 100 or 1000 and you decide to add them up?

The best way is to use a loop. Look at this example:

Example: 10.3

```
1.  <!DOCTYPE HTML PUBLIC "-//W3C//DTD HTML 4.01 Transitional//EN"
    "http://www.w3.org/TR/html4/loose.dtd">
2.  <html>
3.  <head>
4.  <title> Sum in Array </title>
5.  <meta http-equiv="Content-Type" content="text/html; charset=iso-8859-1">
6.  <style type="text/css">
7.  <!--
8.  body{background-color: yellow;
9.  color: blue;
10. text-align: center;
11. border-style:  dotted;
12. width: 150px;}
13. -->
14. </style>
15. <script language="JavaScript" type="text/javascript">
16. <!--
17. var n=0;
18. var sum=0;
19. var number=new
    Array(40,60,70,100,90,65.5);
20. for(n=0;n<6;n++){
21. document.write(number[n]+"<br>");
22. sum +=number[n];
```

```
23. }
24. document.write("<br>Sum of numbers:
    "+sum);
25. -->
26. </script>
27. </head>
28. <body>
29. </body>
30. </html>
```

```
40
60
70
100
90
65.5

Sum of numbers:
425.5
```

In the above example, you see the loop n < 6; which means we know how many elements are stored in our array, in this case, 6 elements. What happens if you do not know how many elements are stored in the array? In this case we use the **length** property.

Array methods
Array provides many methods and properties that help make work more efficient. The most useful properties are **.length, .value** and some methods like **sort()** and **reverse()**.

Use this code, you see it produces an output the same as the above.

```
<script language="JavaScript" type="text/javascript">
 var n=0;
var number=new
Array(40,60,70,100,90,65.5);
for(n=0; n< number.length; n++)
{
document.write(number[n]+"<br>");
}
</script>
```

```
40
60
70
100
90
65.5
```

Sort elements
The sort method provides an excellent means of sorting data. By calling the sort method, all data will be ordered in ascending order (top to bottom). In ascending order the elements will be sorted in alphabetical order from **a** to **z**. The ascending order sorts numbers from smallest to biggest. How you can you sort data in descending order? It is easy to sort data according to descending order.
  ▶ Use ascending order by using **sort ()** method.
  ▶ Use **reverse ()** method to sort in reverse, which is descending order.

Example: 10.4

1. <!DOCTYPE HTML PUBLIC "-//W3C//DTD HTML 4.01 Transitional//EN" "http://www.w3.org/TR/html4/loose.dtd">
2. <html>
3. <head>
4. <title> Ascending and Descending </title>
5. <meta http-equiv="Content-Type" content="text/html; charset=iso-8859-1">
6. <style type="text/css">
7. <!--
8. body{background-color: yellow;
9. color: blue;
10. text-align: center;
11. border-style: dotted;
12. width: 210px;}
13. -->
14. </style>
15. </head>
16. <body>
17. <script language="JavaScript" type="text/javascript">
18. <!--
19. var number=new Array(100,200,30,50,35,75,500,10)
20. var i=0;
21. document.write("Original Numbers
----------------");
22. for (i = 0; i < number.length; i++)
23. {
24. document.write("<br>"+number[i]);
25. }
26. document.write("

Ascending order sort:");
27. document.write("<br>"+number.sort());
28. document.write("

Descending order sort:");
29. document.write("<br>"+number.reverse());
30. -->
31. </script>
32. </body>
33. </html>

```
Original Numbers
----------------
100
200
30
50
35
75
500
10

Ascending order sort:
10,100,200,30,35,50,500,75

Descending order sort:
75,500,50,35,30,200,100,10
```

We can do the same with string array, look at an example.

```
<style type="text/css">
<!--
body{background-color: yellow;
```

```
  color: blue;
  text-align: center;
  width: 300px;
  border-left-style:  ridge;
  border-left-color:maroon;
  border-left-width:20px;

  border-right-style:  ridge;
 border-right-color:maroon;
  border-right-width:20px;

  border-top-style:  ridge;
  border-top-color:yellow;
  border-top-width:20px;


  border-bottom-style:  ridge;
  border-bottom-color:yellow;
  border-bottom-width:20px;
  }
  -->
</style>
</head>
<body>
<script language="JavaScript" type="text/javascript">
<!--
var fruit=new Array("Banana", "Grapes", "Orange", "Angoor", "Balang")
var i=0;
document.write("Original Names<br>----------------");
   for (i = 0; i < fruit.length; i++)
   {
    document.write("<br>"+fruit[i]);
   }
 document.write("<br><br>Ascending order sort:");
 document.write("<br>"+fruit.sort());
 document.write("<br><br>Descending order sort:");
 document.write("<br>"+fruit.reverse());
-->
</script>
</body>
```

More methods

There are other methods that allow using arrays more efficiently. These methods are designed to work in JavaScript. For example the **concat()** method concatenates elements inside the array, and the **join()** method join all element into one string. Here are some useful methods:

Method		Property
concat()	sort()	index
join()	slice()	input
pop()	toSource()	prototype
push()	toString()	length
reverse()	valueOf	
shift()	unshift()	

String object

What is a string? A string is nothing more than a collection of characters. When you develop your website with JavaScript, in many cases you will be forced to use strings. JavaScript provides some elegant ways to manipulate strings. It comes with many methods that allow you to work more efficiently with strings.

String declaration

Declaring strings is the same as any other variable declaration. You can simply declare it as:

```
var string1=" Life is beautiful.";
var string2 =" Not for everyone!";
```

Some useful methods in string object

Method	Description
anchor()	To create an HTML anchor
big()	Big text size
blink()	String blinking
bold()	Bold string
charAt()	Returns the character at a defined position, charAt(10)
charCodeAt()	Returns the Unicode character at a defined position
concat()	Concatenating strings
fixed()	Displays a string as teletype text
fontcolor()	Color string
fontsize()	String font size
indexOf()	Index of specified value
italics()	Italic text
lastIndexOf()	Last part of index
link()	String as a hyperlink
match()	Searches in a string
replace()	Replaces specified characters with some other characters
search()	Searches for values in a string
slice()	Slicing string
small()	Small font
split()	Splits a string into an array of strings
strike()	In a strike format
sub()	Subscript
substr()	A specified number of characters in a string
substring()	Characters in a string between two specified indices
sup()	Superscript
toLowerCase()	Return to lowercase letters
toUpperCase()	Return to uppercase letters
toSource()	The source code of an string object
valueOf()	The primitive value of a String object

String length
To identify the size of a string you can use the string **length( )** method.

Example: 10.5
1. <!DOCTYPE HTML PUBLIC "-//W3C//DTD HTML 4.01 Transitional//EN"
   "http://www.w3.org/TR/html4/loose.dtd">
2. <html>
3. <head>
4. <title> String Size </title>
5. <meta http-equiv="Content-Type" content="text/html; charset=iso-8859-1">
6. <style type="text/css">

7. <!--
8. body{background-color: yellow;
9. color: blue;
10. text-align: center;
11. border-style: dotted;
12. width: 150px;}
13. -->
14. </style>
15. <script language="JavaScript" type="text/javascript">
16. <!--
17. var str ="An eye for eye only ends up making the whole world blind.- Gandhi "
18. document.write("String contains "+str.length+" characters");
19. -->
20. </script>
21. </head>
22. <body>
23. </body>
24. </html>

```
String contains 66
    characters
```

Upper and Lowercases

The method of **toUpperCase()** returns characters in the form of upper case and the method of **toLowerCase()** does the reverse.

```
<script language="JavaScript" type="text/javascript">
    <!--
var st r="A lie gets halfway around the world before the truth has a chance to get its pants
on.-  Winston Churchill (1874-1965)";
document.write("Size of string is "+str.length+" characters<br>");
document.write("See Sting in Upper case!<br>"+str.toUpperCase());
    -->
</script>
```

```
Size of string is 118 characters
See Sting in Upper case!
A LIE GETS HALFWAY AROUND THE WORLD BEFORE THE TRUTH HAS A CHANCE TO GET ITS
PANTS ON.- WINSTON CHURCHILL (1874-1965)
```

String fonts and color methods

There are two really useful string methods: **fontsize()** and **fontcolor()**.
var Msg="Every man is guilty of all the good he didn't do. (Voltaire)!";
var target = Msg.**toUpperCase()**;
document.write ("
The **fontcolor** \"blue\" --> " + Msg.fontcolor("blue"));
document.write ("
The **fontsize** 3 --> " + Msg.fontsize("3"));

The above code creates a font color of blue and a font size of 5.

We try to put more useful string method in an example.

Example: 10.6

```
1.  <!DOCTYPE HTML PUBLIC "-//W3C//DTD HTML 4.01 Transitional//EN"
    "http://www.w3.org/TR/html4/loose.dtd">
2.  <html>
3.  <head>
4.  <title> String Size </title>
5.  <meta http-equiv="Content-Type" content="text/html; charset=iso-8859-1">
6.  <style type="text/css">
       <!--
7.  div{background-color: yellow;
8.  color: maroon;
9.  text-align: center;
10. border-style:  dotted;
11. width:600px}
       -->
12. </style>
13. </head>
14. <body>
15. <div>
16. <script language="JavaScript" type="text/javascript">
        <!--
17. var Msg="Every man is guilty of all the good he didn't do. (Voltaire)!";
18. var target=Msg.toUpperCase();
19. var size=1;
20. var i=0;
21. for ( i=0;i<Msg.length;i++)
22. {
23. document.write(target.charAt(i).fontsize(size).bold())
24. if (size<5)
25. size++;
26. else
27. size=1
28. }
29. document.write ("<p>The big() --> " + Msg.big());
30. document.write ("<br>The small() --> " + Msg.small());
31. document.write ("<br>The bold() -->" + Msg.bold());
32. document.write ("<br>The fixed() --> " + Msg.fixed());
33. document.write ("<br>The fontcolor \"blue\" --> " + Msg.fontcolor("blue"));
34. document.write ("<br>The fontsize 3 --> " + Msg.fontsize("3"));
35. document.write ("<br>The strike() --> " + Msg.strike());
36. document.write ("<br>The sub() --> " + Msg.sub());
37. document.write ("<br>The sup() --> " + Msg.sup());
```

38. document.write ("
The blink() --> " + Msg.blink()); // Doesn't work on IE
        -->
39. </script>
40. </div>
41. </body>
42. </html>

The method **charAt()** reads a character from a string according to the specified index number. For example charAt(0); will read the **E** letter.

More string methods
There are more string methods that help us to manipulate strings. Some methods act very similar, like **substr()** and **substring()** method. The difference between them is that substring() takes two arguments, **start**, **end**. For example substring(1,5), which means take chuck of string from index of 1 to 5, on the other hand the substr(1,5) starts from I and takes 5 characters.

About substring
If the start-index is equal to the stop-index, the result will be an empty string.
If you do not specify the stop-index, it takes from the start-index to the end of the string.
If the start-index is greater than the stop-index, then the substring function swaps 2 arguments.

var Msg="Every man is guilty of all the good he didn't do. (Voltaire)!";
document.write ("<p>The substring() --> " + Msg.substring(6,9));
document.write ("<p>The substr() --> " + Msg.substr(6,9));

Review questions

1-var number[0]="peter"; is this declaration correct?

2-var names=new Array("Peter", "Bob", Jack", Isabelle"); what is the index of Bob?

3- Array is a keyword   True   False

4- var number = new Array(40,60,70,100,90,65.5);

On the above array how do you add 60 and 90?

5- var number = new Array(40,60,70,100,90,65.5); sort this array.

6- var number = new Array(40,60,70,100,90,65.5); sort this array in descending order.

7- var number = new Array(40,60,70,100,90,65.5); how do you find the size of this array?

8- var string1=" Life is beautiful."; string1.charAt(0) produce-------------------------------

9-What is the difference between substring () and substr()?

10- In substring, If the start-index is equal to the stop-index, what will be the result?

Answer

1-Yes it is correct

2- 1

3- True

4- var sum = number[1]+number[4];

5-number.sort()

6- after sorting use number.reverse()

7-number.lenght

8- L

9- substring() counts from start to stop index, substr counts from start-index and goes according to the second argument. For example substr(2,10) , starts at index 2 and outputs 10 characters.

Chapter 11

Introduction

Form is the most important part of web design. You will rarely see a website that does not use forms. The form builder is totally done by HTML but here we do not talk about how to create a form, rather our intention relates to JavaScript and how to validate a form. Form validation is a technique that prevents possible mistakes that a user may be faced with. It makes programs smarter.

Validating forms

What is form validation? Form validation is the procedure that validates user data. When a user enters information into a textbox, JavaScript then validates the information before sending it to the sever-side. Some examples of form validation are:

- It should send a message if the field is left empty.
- It should validate the email.
- It should validate alphanumeric for addresses.
- It should validate the date.
- It should distinguish difference between character and numeric.
- It should validate the size of password or size of user name.
- It should be able to distinguish between upper and lowercase letter.

There are two ways to validate data:
- Client-side using JavaScript.
- Server-side using **PHP** or **Perl**.

On the client-side we validate the data before sending it to the server-side, so data gets validated faster. On the other hand we can validate data using PHP on the server-side. Here we do form validation with JavaScript on the client side. We will bring many examples of HTML form and JavaScript codes together.

Client Validation	Server Validation
Validate data before sending it. If data is not correct, then warning you! using JavaScript to validate data in client side!	Validate data after sending. If data is not correct it, then warning you! using PHP to validate data in server side!

We generate textboxes such as: text field, text area, radio, check box, list, drop down list or combo box. The textboxes allow communication with servers and especially with our databases.

The simple HTML form can be like this:

```
<form>
<input type="text" name= "input_box" value="Enter your name here!">
</form>
```

The above code generates this text box and allows a user to enter their name.

Input your name: Enter your name here!

Before using form validation, let's work on the HTML form and JavaScript. Here we try to simply add two numbers. You will use text fields to enter number 1 and number 2, and then we will use another text field to handle the total numbers.

Contents of a form

▶ A form must have a name, as in:
  <form **name**="adding">
▶ Text boxes must have a name, as in:
  Number One: <INPUT TYPE = "Text" **NAME** = "Number1" SIZE = 10 value ="">
▶ The output box must have a name like:
  Show total: <INPUT TYPE = "Text" **NAME** = "total" SIZE = 10 value = "">
▶ Put a function into JavaScript code like this:

```
function calculate()
{
A = document.frmAdd.Number1.value
B = document.frmAdd.Number2.value
C = (A + B)
 document.frmAdd.total.value=C
}
```

Example: 11.1

```
1.  <!DOCTYPE HTML PUBLIC "-//W3C//DTD HTML 4.01 Transitional//EN"
    "http://www.w3.org/TR/html4/loose.dtd">
2.  <html>
3.  <head>
4.  <title> HTML Form and JavaScript </title>
5.  <meta http-equiv="Content-Type" content="text/html; charset=iso-8859-1">
6.  <style type="text/css">
7.  <!--
8.  div{
9.  background-color: yellow;
10. color: maroon;
11. border-left-color:maroon;
12. text-align: center;
13. font-weight: bold;
14. border-style:  ridge;
15. width:200px;
16. border-width:10px;
17. }
18. -->
19. </style>
20. <script language="JavaScript" type="text/javascript">
21. <!--
22. function calculate() {
23. num1 = document.frmAdd.Number1.value
24. num2= document.frmAdd.Number2.value
25. sum = (num1 + num2)
26.  document.frmAdd.total.value=sum
27. }
28. -->
29. </script>
30. </head>
31. <body>
32. <div>
33. <FORM NAME = frmAdd>
34. Number One: <INPUT TYPE = "Text" NAME = "Number1" SIZE = 10 value ="">
35. Number Two: <INPUT TYPE = "Text" NAME = "Number2" SIZE = 10 value ="">
36. <P>
37. Show total: <INPUT TYPE = "Text" NAME = "total" SIZE = 10 value = "">
38. <P>
39. <Input Type = "Button" NAME = "BT1" VALUE = "Add them" onClick = calculate()>
40. </FORM>
41. </div>
42. </body>
43. </html>
```

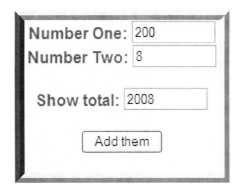

▶ **Whoops!** 200 + 8 equals 208 and not 2008, so what went wrong? It actually did not add the two numbers; rather it joined (concatenated) two numbers.

The reality is, problems come from textboxes. By default everything you input into the textbox will be treated as **string** (*text*), therefore JavaScript thinks that it must to concatenate two strings.

Solution
You must return the numbers to be treated as numeric values, not as string; in this case we have a few options:

▶ Use **Number()** method to return the string into numbers like this:

num1=Number(num1);
num2=Number(num2);

▶ We can use the JavaScript function **eval()**. The eval() function converts a string to numbers.

num1 = eval(document.frmAdd.Number1.value)
num2 = eval(document.frmAdd.Number2.value)

▶ Parse them to **Float** like this:
num1=parseFloat(num1);
num2=parseFloat(num2);

▶ Parse them to **Integer** like this:
num1=parseFloat(num1);
num2=parseFloat(num2);

Example: 11.2
1. <!DOCTYPE HTML PUBLIC "-//W3C//DTD HTML 4.01 Transitional//EN" "http://www.w3.org/TR/html4/loose.dtd">
2. <html>
3. <head>
4. <title> HTML Form and JavaScript Correction </title>
5. <meta http-equiv="Content-Type" content="text/html; charset=iso-8859-1">
6. <style type="text/css">
7. <!--
8. div{
9. background-color: yellow;
10. color: maroon;

```
11. border-left-color:maroon;
12. text-align: center;
13. font-weight: bold;
14. border-style:  ridge;
15. width:200px;
16. border-width:10px;
17. }
18. -->
19. </style>
20. <script language="JavaScript" type="text/javascript">
21. <!--
22. function calculate() {
23. num1 = document.frmAdd.Number1.value
24. num2= document.frmAdd.Number2.value
25. num1=Number(num1);
26. num2=Number(num2);
27. sum = (num1 + num2);
28. document.frmAdd.total.value=sum
29. }
30. -->
31. </script>
32. </head>
33. <body>
34. <div>
35. <FORM NAME = frmAdd>
36. Number One: <INPUT TYPE = "Text" NAME = "Number1" SIZE = 10 value ="">
37. Number Two: <INPUT TYPE = "Text" NAME = "Number2" SIZE = 10 value ="">
38. <P>
39. Show total: <INPUT TYPE = "Text" NAME = "total" SIZE = 10 value = "">
40. <P>
41. <Input Type = "Button" NAME = "BT1" VALUE = "Add them" onClick = calculate()>
42. </FORM>
43. </div>
44. </body>
45. </html>
```

How we fixed the problems

▶ You can use **Number()** method:

num1=Number(num1);
num2=Number(num2);

▶ You may also use **eval()** method:

Num1 = eval(document.frmAdd.Number1.value)

num2 = eval(document.frmAdd.Number2.value)

> ▶ Parse them to **Float** like this:

num1=parseFloat(num1);
num2=parseFloat(num2);

> ▶ Parse them to **Integer** like this:

num1=parseFloat(num1);
num2=parseFloat(num2);

Carefully look at the form and its relationship with JavaScript code.

<FORM **NAME** = frmAdd>

Number One: <INPUT TYPE = "Text" **NAME** = "Number1" SIZE = 10 value ="">

The form has a name, which is **frmAdd**, and the text box has a name, which is **Number1**.

Now look at the JavaScript **function calculate()**. Under this function you see

num1 = document.frmAdd.Number1.value

num1 =	document	.frmAdd	.Number1	.value
⇧	⇧	⇧	⇧	⇧
Variable	**Document**	**Name of form**	**Name of textbox**	**Value property Read and write**

In order to complete the mathematical function and form implementation we use another example that calculates the square root of a given number.

Example: 11.3

1. <!DOCTYPE HTML PUBLIC "-//W3C//DTD HTML 4.01 Transitional//EN" "http://www.w3.org/TR/html4/loose.dtd">
2. <html>
3. <head>
4. <title> Calculate Square Roots </title>
5. <meta http-equiv="Content-Type" content="text/html; charset=iso-8859-1">
6. <style type="text/css">
7. <!--
8. div{background-color: yellow;
9. color: maroon;
10. text-align: center;
11. border-style: dotted;
12. width:250px}
13. -->

```
14. </style>
15. </head>
16. <body>
17. <script language="JavaScript" type="text/javascript">
18. <!--
19. function compute(form) {
20. form.sqr.value = Math.sqrt(eval(form.num.value));
21. }
22. -->
23. </script>
24. <BODY>
25. <div>
26. <FORM NAME="evalform">
27. Enter number: <INPUT TYPE="text" NAME="num" value="">
28. Square: <INPUT TYPE="text" NAME="sqr" value="">
29. <INPUT TYPE="button" VALUE="Square It" onClick="compute(this.form)">
30. </FORM>
31. </div>
32. </BODY>
33. </HTML>
```

Enter number: 8
Square: 2.8284271247461903
Square It

Textbox input/output

The idea of validating textboxes is to prevent users from entering wrong data into a textbox. We have to predict what kind of mistakes a user can make, therefore we try to block it and send a message to the user and alert them about the problem. For example a user must not enter characters in the age textbox and should not enter numerals instead of the name. Let's look at an example of input and output using a textbox (text field).

Example: 11.4

```
1.   <HTML>
2.   <HEAD>
3.   <title> Textboxes input/output </title>
4.   <meta http-equiv="Content-Type" content="text/html; charset=iso-8859-1">
5.   <SCRIPT type="text/javascript">
6.   <!--
7.   function InOut()
8.   {
9.   var str="";
```

10. str+="First Name:"+document.Frm.fname.value+"\r";
11. str+="Lsat Name:"+document.Frm.lname.value+"\r";
12. str+="First Name length:"+document.Frm.fname.value.length+"\r";
13. str+="LLast Name length:"+document.Frm.lname.value.length;
14. alert(str);
15. }
16. -->
17. </SCRIPT>
18. </HEAD>
19. <BODY>
20. <FORM NAME="Frm" action="">
21. First Name:
22. <INPUT TYPE="text" NAME="fname"><p>
23. Last Name:
24. <INPUT TYPE="text" NAME="lname"><p>
25. <INPUT TYPE="button" VALUE="Submit" onClick="InOut()">
26. </FORM>
27. </BODY>
28. </HTML>

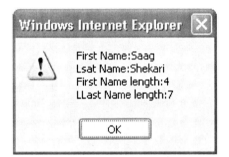

Textbox validation

We check if textboxes are left empty. If the user forgets to input a textbox it will send a message "Please insert in the text box". We can change the color of the background if the textbox is empty. You can use **focus()** to put the cursor in a certain place so that the user knows which textbox has to be filled.

Example: 11.5

1. <!DOCTYPE HTML PUBLIC "-//W3C//DTD HTML 4.01 Transitional//EN"
   "http://www.w3.org/TR/html4/loose.dtd">
2. <html>
3. <head>
4. <title> Form Validation Check Empty Textbox </title>
5. <meta http-equiv="Content-Type" content="text/html; charset=iso-8859-1">
6. <style type="text/css" media="screen">
7. <!--
8. body{

```
9.   margin: 5px auto;
10.  background:white;
11.  font-family:arial;
12.  }
13.  table{
14.  display:block;
15.  margin: 0px auto;
16.  background:yellow;
17.  color:blue;
18.  font-weight:bold;
19.  border-style:  ridge;
20.  border-width:10px;
21.  }
22.  -->
23.  </style>
24.  <script language="javascript" type="text/javascript">
25.  <!--
26.  function validateTextboxes(Chkform)
27.  {
28.  if(""==document.Chkform.fullName.value)
29.  {
30.  document.Chkform.fullName.style.background = '#eeeeee';
31.  document.Chkform.fullName.focus();
32.  alert("Please enter your full name.");
33.  return false;
34.  }
35.  if(" "==document.Chkform.email.value)
36.  {
37.  document.Chkform.email.style.background = '#eeeeee';
38.  document.Chkform.email.focus();
39.  alert("Please enter your email address.");
40.  return false;
41.  }
42.  return 0 }
43.  -->
44.  </script>
45.  </head>
46.  <body>
47.  <form name="Chkform" method="" action="" onSubmit="return
     validateTextboxes(Chkform);">
48.  <table border="1">
49.  <tr>
50.  <td>Full Name:</td>
51.  <td><input type="text" name="fullName" length="20"></td>
52.  </tr>
53.  <tr>
```

54. `<td>Email:</td>`
55. `<td><input type="text" name="email" length="20"></td>`
56. `</tr>`
57. `<tr>`
58. `<td><input type="submit" name="submit" value="Submit"></td>`
59. `<td><input type="reset" name="reset"></td>`
60. `</tr>`
61. `</table>`
62. `</form>`
63. `</body>`
64. `</html>`

Validate string length

Sometimes you need to have some limitation on the text length, for example if you want the user names to be no greater than 10 and no less than 4 characters. We use the length property to have control over the size of string.

```
<script language="javascript" type="text/javascript">
<!--
function validateTextboxes(Chkform)
{
if ((document.Chkform.fullName.value.length< 4) ||
(document.Chkform.fullName.value.length > 10))
 {
   error = "Length of name must be between 4 to 10.\n";
   alert(error);
}
return true;
}
<tr>
<td>Full Name:</td>
<td><input type="text" name="fullName" length="20"></td>
</tr>
<tr>
<td><input type="submit" name="submit" value="Submit"></td>
<td><input type="reset" name="reset"></td>
</tr>
```

Numerical validation

We must check our text box to see if the user has entered a numeric value or string. For example if the user must enter his or her age, we have to check to ensure that the value entered is a number and not a string. The easiest way to check for numeric value is to use the JavaScript built-in function **isNaN()**. The isNaN() stands for "is not a number". It accepts an argument, the value of the field named in the form. If this value is not numeric, validation fails.

```
<script language="javascript" type="text/javascript">
<!--
function validateTextboxes(Chkform)
{
if (isNaN(document.Chkform.num.value))
{
alert("Please enter a numeric value
only!");
return false;
}
return true
}
 -->
</script> </head> <body>
```

```
<form name="Chkform" method="" action="" onSubmit="return validate Textboxes
(Chkform); " >
<table border="1">
<tr> <td>Enter Age:</td>
<td><input type="text" name="num" length="20"></td>
</tr> <tr>
<td><input type="submit" name="submit" value="Submit"></td>
<td><input type="reset" name="reset"></td>
</tr>  </table> </form> </body>
</html>
```

Validating the @ character

We use JavaScript's **indexOf()** method to validate the @ character. It simply searches for substring until it finds the exact character. In this case it is looking for the '@' character. It starts searching from the index of zero. If nothing is found then returns to -1, meaning validation has failed.

```
var mail = Chkform.email.value
if (mail.indexOf('@') < 0)
{
alert("Please enter a valid Email");
return false;
}
```

You must use the' @' character instead of '#'.

Email validation

The above validation is a basic email validation, but JavaScript gives us more flexibility to validate the data in advanced format. We can use the method of string which we learned on the previous chapter, as in indexOf(). We can validate every piece of the email. For example some important validations are:
  ▶ Make sure the mail box is not empty
  ▶ If the @ is included
  ▶ If the dot '.' is included
  ▶ If after the dot there are two or three characters
  ▶ If after the @ there are some characters
  ▶ Check for some characters like **#, $, %,** ^, **&,** *, **{,)** and so on which should not be included.
  ▶ The semi-colon must not be present
  ▶ The comma must not be included (sometimes users make a mistake – instead of pressing a dot they may press comma).
  ▶ Check for white-space
  ▶ Check for double '@'
  ▶ To validate Radio button, Checkbox, Text area and the like

Example: 11.6

```
1.  <!DOCTYPE HTML PUBLIC "-//W3C//DTD HTML 4.01 Transitional//EN"
    "http://www.w3.org/TR/html4/loose.dtd">
2.  <html>
3.  <head>
4.  <title> Email Validation </title>
5.  <meta http-equiv="Content-Type" content="text/html; charset=iso-8859-1">
6.  <script language="javascript" type="text/javascript">
7.  <!--
8.  function validateTextboxes(Chkform) {
9.  if (document.Chkform.email.value.length == 0) {
10. document.Chkform.email.style.background = 'yellow';
11. alert("Please enter an Email address!");
12. return false;
13. }
14. if (document.Chkform.email.value.indexOf("@") <0) {
15. document.Chkform.email.style.background = 'green';
16. alert("The '@' is missing \r Please enter the @ character \rat an appropriate
    place!");
17. return false;
18. }
19. if (document.Chkform.email.value.indexOf("\.") < 0) {
20. document.Chkform.email.style.background = 'gray';
21. alert("E-mail address is missing a dot '.'");
22. return false;
23. }
24. if (document.Chkform.email.value.indexOf(":") > -1) {
25. document.Chkform.email.style.background = 'blue';
26. alert("E-mail must not contian this ':' invalid  colon\r Please remove colon");
27. return false;
28. }
29. if (document.Chkform.email.value.indexOf(",") > -1) {
30. document.Chkform.email.style.background = 'red';
31. alert("E-mail address must not contian a comma ',' \rPlease remove the comma");
32. return false;
33. }
34. if (document.Chkform.email.value.indexOf(";") > -1) {
35. document.Chkform.email.style.background = 'yellow';
36. alert("E-mail address must not contian a semi-colon ';'\rPlease remove the semi-
    colon ");
37. return false;
38. }
39. if (document.Chkform.email.value.indexOf("/") > -1) {
40. document.Chkform.email.style.background = 'green';
41. alert("E-mail address has an invalid slash '/'character \rPlease remove the forward
    slash!");
```

42. return false;
43. }
44. if (document.Chkform.email.value.indexOf("#") > -1) {
45. document.Chkform.email.style.background = 'gray';
46. alert("E-mail address must not contian a pound '#' \r Please remove this # character ");
47. return false;
48. }
49. return true;
50. }
51. -->
52. </script>
53. </head>
54. <body>
55. <form name="Chkform" method="" action="" onSubmit="return validateTextboxes(Chkform);">
56. <table border="1">
57. <tr>
58. <td>Email:</td>
59. <td><input type="text" name="email" length="20"></td>
60. </tr>
61. <tr>
62. <td><input type="submit" name="submit" value="Submit"></td>
63. <td><input type="reset" name="reset" value="Clear"></td>
64. </tr>
65. </table>
66. </form>
67. </body>
68. </html>

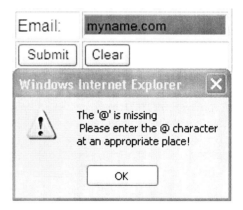

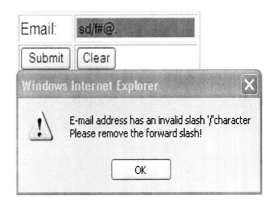

Checkbox validation

We check the checkboxes if at least one of them has been checked. In fact we remind the users to check one or more of the required checkboxes.

```
<script language=javascript>
function validateCheckBox(chk){
if (document.chk.chk1.checked == false &&
document.chk.chk2.checked == false) {
alert("Please select at least one checkbox.\n");
return false;
}
  else
 alert("Thank you!")
}
</script>
</head>
<body>
Please check one or more boxes:
<form name="chk" action="">
<input type=checkbox name=chk1>Box 1
<input type=checkbox name=chk2>Box 2
<p><input type=button name="but" value="Check" onclick="return
validateCheckBox(chk);">
</form>
</body>
</html>
```

Radio buttons

The radio button is the same as the checkbox except that only one radio is allowed to be checked at one time. If one check is true then the rest will be in the false states. The index of the first radio is always zero and it will increases by one. For example the first radio index=0, second radio index=1 and so on.

Example: 11.7

```
1.  <html>
2.  <script language="javascript" type="text/javascript">
3.  <!--
4.  function validateRadio(Chkform){
5.  var index=0;
6.  for (var i=0; i<document.Chkform.R1.length; i++) {
7.  if (document.Chkform.R1[i].checked == true)  {
8.  index++;
9.  break; }
10. }
11. if (index == 0) {
12. alert("Please check a radio button.");
13. return false; }
14. else
15. alert("You checked:  "+document.Chkform.R1[i].value.toUpperCase());
16. return true; }
17. -->
18. </script> </head> <body>
19. <form name="Chkform" method="" action="" onSubmit="return
      validateRadio(Chkform);">
20. <table border="1">
21. <tr> <td><input type="radio" name = "R1" value = "Horse"> Horse</td>
22. <td><input type="radio" name = "R1" value = "Camel"> Camel </td>
```

23. `<td><input type="radio" name = "R1" value = "Cow"> Cow</td>`
24. `</tr> <tr>`
25. `<td><input type="submit" name="submit" value="Submit"></td>`
26. `<td><input type="reset" name="reset" value="Clear"></td>`
27. `</tr>`
28. `</table> </form> </body>`
29. `</html>`

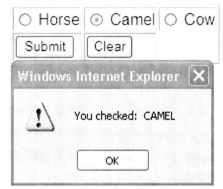

Password validation

To validate the password box you may need to check something like:

▸ Check the length of the password
▸ Check for white spaces (not allowed)
▸ Check if box is not empty
▸ Check if the second password is exactly the same as first entry
▸ Check for numeric of alphanumeric
▸ Check if at least one character is in uppercase (option)

Example: 11.8

1. `<!DOCTYPE HTML PUBLIC "-//W3C//DTD HTML 4.01 Transitional//EN"`
   `"http://www.w3.org/TR/html4/loose.dtd">`
2. `<html>`
3. `<head>`
4. `<title> Radio Validation </title>`
5. `<meta http-equiv="Content-Type" content="text/html; charset=iso-8859-1">`
6. `<script language="javascript" type="text/javascript">`
7. `<!--`
8. `function validatePassword() {`
9. `var space = " ";// used for white space`
10. `var minLength = 5;`
11. `var pwd1 = document.Chkform.password1.value;`
12. `var pwd2 = document.Chkform.password2.value;`
13. `if (pwd1 == " " || pwd2 == ") {`

```
14. alert('Please enter your password!');
15. return false; }
16. if (document.Chkform.password1.value.indexOf(space) > -1) {
17. alert("White spaces are not allowed.");
18. return false; }
19. if (document.Chkform.password1.value.length < minLength) {
20. alert('Password must be ' + minLength + ' characters long. Try again.');
21. return false; }
22. else {
23. if (pwd1 != pwd2) {
24. alert ("Both password entry must be the same!.");
25. return false; }
26. else {
27. alert('We varified your password\r Both password are the same!');
28. return true;      }
29. }
30. }
31. -->
32. </script>
33. </HEAD>
34. <body>
35. <form name="Chkform" method="" action="" onSubmit="return validatePassword
    (Chkform); ">
36. <table border="1">
37. <tr>
38. <td>Password:</td><td> <input type=password name=password1
    maxlength=10></td>
39. </tr> <tr>
40. <td>Confirm password:</td><td> <input type=password name=password2
    maxlength=10></td>
41. </tr> <tr>
42. <td><input type="submit" name="submit" value="Submit"></td>
43. <td><input type="reset" name="reset" value="Clear"></td>
44. </tr>
45. </table> </form> </body>
46. </html>
```

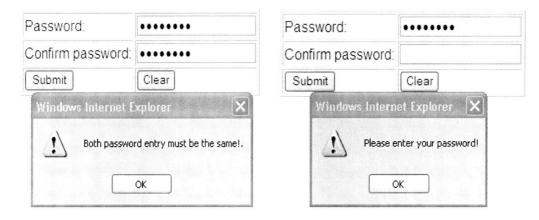

In many cases we validate boxes with the regular expression; please check the regular expression for your future studies.

Review questions

1.   What is form validation?
2.   We can validate a form on the client-side or server-side   True   False
3.   How do you parse a number, for example to float?
4.   What does the focus method do?
5.   What does this statement do?
if ((document.Chkform.text.value.length< 4) || (document.Chkform.text.value.length > 10))
6.   What is **isNaN**?
7.   What happens if you do not validate a form?
8.   What major validating should be used for email?
9.   This statement creates a reset button<input type="reset" name="reset" value="Clear"> True   False
10. Can we create a form with combination of CSS, HTML and JavaScript?
    Yes   No

Answer

1.   Validating a form blocks the user from entering wrong data. For example instead of name they should not input a number.
2.   True
3.   num1=parseFloat(num1);
4.   The focus method bring the cursor to the related textbox (focus target)
5.   Binds length to be no less than 4 characters and no longer than 10 characters
6.   Stand for "Is Not a Number", and we use it to validate numerical values
7.   User may enter wrong data
8.   You should validate the @ and the dot[.]
9.   True
10. Yes

Chapter 12

Introduction

JavaScript events are really essential to web design programming. They provide an easy way to manage the code. In fact events are small methods that trigger the JavaScript code. We usually click on a button and following our click the event takes place. In this chapter we try to look at windows operations like resizing and moving windows, the navigator and status. We will also looking at cookies and their impact on a browser. In this chapter some examples are checked with both browsers – Firefox and IE7.0.

JavaScript events

What is an event? An event is an essential part of JavaScript. In fact it is just a small method that triggers the script. Events are placed outside of JavaScript, usually on the HTML part, and allow to be clicked. Some events wait for a mouse to be clicked, such as **onClick()**, while others act automatically, such as **onLoad()**.

In some previous chapters we have used JavaScript events without mentioning the event word like **onMouseOver, onClick(), onLoad(), onSubmit()**, and so on. Events make JavaScript dynamic, allowing users to do some operations live on the web page.

Here is a list of some important event that you usually use when building your website.

Event name	Description
onAbort	Aborts an image from loading
onFocus	Focuses on the text box
onChange	Data will be changed by user
onClick	Waiting for user click
onDblClick	Acts when user clicks twice
onDragDrop	An icon is dragged and dropped into the browser

onError	Acts usually when JavaScript error occurs
onBlur	Reverse of the focus, loses focus
onKeyDown	User press a key
onKeyPress	Acts when a user presses or holds down a key.
onKeyUp	Acts when a user releases a key.
onLoad	Automatically load acts when page loads
onMouseDown	Acts when user presses a mouse button.
onMouseMove	Acts when user moves the mouse.
onMouseOut	Acts when mouse leaves the button
onMouseOver	Acts when mouse is placed on the button(without clicking)
onMouseUp	Acts when user releases a mouse button.
onMove	Acts when user moves a window frame.
onReset	Clear all boxes
onResize	Allows a user to resize window or window frame.
onSelect	Allows a user to select text within the field.
onSubmit	Acts when user presses submit
onUnload	Acts when user leaves the page

onLoad event

The onload event causes an action to load along with the page loading. When you use the onload event the action does not wait for the user to click. It automatically loads the related action. Look at this example.

Example: 12.1

```
1.  <html> <head>
2.  <title> OnLoad </title>
3.  <script type="text/javascript">
4.  <!--
5.  function Events() {
6.  var output="";
7.  var right_now=new Date();
8.  output+= right_now.getDate()+":";
9.  output+= right_now.getMonth()+1+":";
10. output+= right_now.getYear();
11. alert("Now is the Leap day!\r
    Day:Month:Year \r"+output); }
12. -->
13. </script>
14. </head>
15. <body onLoad = "Events()">
16. </body></html>
```

The program does not wait for the user to click. As soon as the page is loaded you see this output. What happens if you change the **onLoad** to **onClick**?

onClick event

Unlike the onLoad event, the onClick event waits for the user to click. Upon the user's click it triggers the related event. We try to change just the **onload** method to **onclick**.

Example: 12.2

When you click on the button it shows the date.

1. <html>
2. <head>
3. <title> onClick </title>
4. <script type="text/javascript">
5. <!--
6. function Events() {
7. var output="";
8. var right_now=new Date();
9. output+=right_now.getDate()+":";
10. output+=right_now.getMonth()+1+":";
11. output+=right_now.getYear();
12. alert("Now is the Leap day!\r
    Day:Month:Year \r"+output);
13. }
14. -->
15. </script>
16. </head>
17. <body>
18. <A HREF="#"**onClick**="Events();">
    Click Me</a>
19. </body></html>

onFocus event

The onFocus event occurs when an input like a textbox, text area or a select option gets focused by keyboard tabbing or by mouse clicking.

onBlur event

The reverse side of **onFocus** is the **onBlur**. It occurs when an input like a textbox, text area or a select option loses its focus. For example if you set **onBlur** for a textbox, click on that textbox and then click anywhere outside of the related textbox, you will see the message related to the onBlur shown on screen.

Example: 12.3

1. <html>
2. <head>
3. <title> onFocus and onBlur</title>
4. <script type="text/javascript">
5. <!--
6. function Events()
7. {
8. alert("Out of focus");

9.   }
10. -->
11. </script>
12. <style type="text/css">
13. <!--
14. div{background-color: yellow;
15. border-width:20px;
16. border-style: ridge;
17. width: 150px;}
18. -->
19. </style></head>
20. <body>
21. <input type="text" name="email"

If you click on the first textbox you see the "***Got focus***" then try to click on the second textbox and click outside of the textbox to see the message.

22. size="20" value="Enter your email address" **onfocus**="this.value='Got focus'">
23. <input type="text" name="name1"
24. size="20" value=""**onBlur**="Events();">
25.   </body></html>

onMouseOver

The *onMouseOver* event is triggered when a user places the cursor over the button.

onMouseOut

The *onMouseOver* event is triggered when the cursor leaves the button or area of event.

Example: 12.4

1.   <html> <head>
2.   <title> MouseOver and MouseOut</title>
3.   <script type="text/javascript">
4.   <!--
5.   function MouseOver() {
6.   document.Mouse.src ="MouseOver.jpg"; }
7.   function MouseOut() {
8.   document.Mouse.src ="MouseOut.jpg"; }
9.   -->
10. </script>
11. <style type="text/css">
12. <!--
13. div{background-color: yellow;
14. border-width:10px;
15. border-style: ridge;
16. width: 150px;}

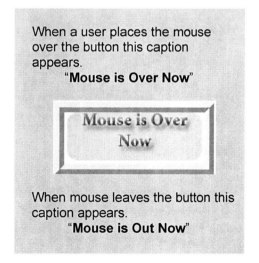

When a user places the mouse over the button this caption appears.
        "**Mouse is Over Now**"

When mouse leaves the button this caption appears.
        "**Mouse is Out Now**"

17. -->
18. </style>
19. </head>
20. <body>
<a href="#" target="_blank"
21. **onmouseover**="MouseOver()" **onmouseout**="MouseOut()">
22. <img border="0" alt="Mouse Events!" src="MouseOut.jpg" name="Mouse"></a>
23. </body></html>

Windows Operating

Windows provides several nice attributes and allows programmers to manage and modify the windows. You can use open, close, width, height, resize and the like. Look at the table of attributes.

Attributes	Description
width	Width in new window like **width=300** (measure is in pixels)
height	height in new window like **height=200** (measure is in pixels)
resizable	Ability to resize the window. **Resizable=yes** or **no**
scrollbars	Create scrollbar, **scrollbars=yes** or **no**
toolbar	Have toolbar or not. **toolbar=yes** or **no**
location	Place of url. **location=yes** or **no**
status	Show status bar. **status=yes** or **no**
menubar	Show menu bar. **menubar=yes** or **no**

You may want to use these options on your new window.
  ▶ **screenX=number** of pixels from the left of the screen
  ▶ **screenY=number** of pixels from the top of the screen
  ▶ **left=number** of pixels from the left of the screen
  ▶ **top=number** of pixels from the left of the screen

There are four predefined targets: "**_blank**", "**_self**", "**_parent** ", and "**_top**".

_blank	To open a new window
_self	To open in current window
_parent	To open in parent window otherwise as self
_top	To open in entire window

Example: 12.5
1. <html>
2. <head>
3. <title> Open Windows </title>
4. <script type="text/javascript">
5. <!--
6. function Wins() {

7.   window.open('http://www.shanbedi.com','640x480','width=300,height=100')}
8.   -->
9.   </script>
10. <style type="text/css">
11. <!--
12. div{background-color: yellow;
13. border-width:10px;
14. border-style: ridge;
15. width: 150px;}
16. -->
17. </style>
18. </head>
19. <body> <form>
20. Open a new simple window in 640 x 480 pixels:
21. <INPUT TYPE=BUTTON VALUE="640x480" onClick="Wins()">
22.
23. </form></body></html>

The above program does not use many attributes except **width** and **height**. Now we use some attributes that are provided by JavaScript. We create a new file with an html extension then we call the new file.

Example: 12.6
Save this file as **new.html**

```
<html>
<head>
<title> Open Windows </title>
</head>
<body>
This is new window<br>
<a href="javascript:self.close()">close window</a>
</body>
</html>
```

Then we write a program to open this file in a new customized window.
We use **<a href="javascript:self.close()">close window</a>** when the user clicks on the close window button the **self.close()** method closes the window.
<html>
<head>
<title> Open Windows </title>
<script type="text/javascript">
<!--
function Wins() {

```
window.open('new.html','640x480','status=yes,scrollbars=yes,location=yes,menubar=yes,
width=200,height=100')}
--> </script>
<style type="text/css">
<!--
div{background-color: yellow;
border-width:10px;
border-style:  ridge;
width: 150px;}
-->
</style> </head>
<body><div><form>
Open new window in 640 x 480 pixels use attributes:
<INPUT TYPE=BUTTON VALUE="640x480" onClick="Wins()">
</div>
</form></body></html>
```

You can use **fullscreen=yes** command to open the new window in the full screen size.

Windows manipulation

When a window is opened then you can do many operations on the open window like Move, Close, resize and the like. There are some methods that may help you to manage the window.

- ▶ **window.location.reload()** //reloads window
- ▶ **window.close()** //closes window
- ▶ **window.moveTo(x,y)** //moves window to exact specified location
- ▶ **window.moveBy(x,y)** // move by a specified distance from their current location.
- ▶ **window.resizeTo(x,y)** //resizes window to specified X,Y
- ▶ **window.resizeBy(x,y)** //resizes window by specified shrink and grow relative to original window.

Note: Do not get confused between **resizeTo()** and **resizeBy()** methods. The resizeTo(x,y)returns to the exact size of window. The resizeBy(x,y) adds to or subtracts from the current dimensions. It never sets absolute dimensions.

In order for a window to be shrinking you can use negative values.
<a href="javascript:window.resizeBy(-50,-50)">
The **availWidth** property returns the width of the display screen without the Windows Taskbar.

Example: 12.7

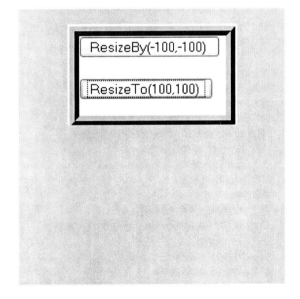

```
1.   <html>
2.   <head>
3.   <title> Resize_BY and  Resize_To </title>
4.   <script type="text/javascript">
5.   <!--
6.   function Resize_BY(){
7.   window.resizeBy(-150,-150);
8.   }
9.   function Resize_To(){
10.  window.resizeTo(window.screen.availWidth/2, window.screen.availHeight/2);
11.  }
12.  -->
13.  </script>
14.  <style type="text/css">
15.  <!--
16.  div{background-color: yellow;
17.  border-width:10px;
18.  border-style:  ridge;
19.  width: 150px;}
20.  -->
21.  </style> </head>
22.  <body><div><form>
23.  <input type="button"
     value="ResizeBy(-100,-100) "
     onClick="Resize_BY();"></br></br>
24.  <input type="button"
     value="ResizeTo(100,100) "
     onClick="Resize_To();">
25.  </div>
26.  </form></body></html>
```

To resize a window to the full size screen you can use this code:
self.resizeTo(screen.width, screen.height);
On the above example you can use the **MoveBY()** and **MoveTo()** methods.
When you use "**self**" or "**this**," as in **self.moveto()**, it refers to the current window.

```
Function Resize_BY() {
window.moveBy(-150,-150);
    }
 function Resize_To() {
self.moveTo(50,100);
    }
```

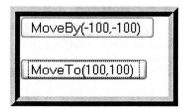

Interactive resizing

By using width and height you can create an interactive resizing. The user inputs into the box (Width, Height) then presses the button. The **value** means an integer number that you entered in the textbox.

Note: the document.all() is old and instead of that you can use **getElemetById**.

Example: 12.8

```
1.   <script type="text/javascript">
2.   <!--
3.   function Resize(x,y) {
4.   window.resizeTo(x,y);
5.   }
6.   function ResizeIt() {
7.   var x = document.all("Width").value;
8.   var y = document.all("Height").value;
9.   Resize(x,y);
10.  }
11.  //-->
12.  </script>
13.  <style type="text/css">
14.  <!--
15.  div{background-color: yellow;
16.  border-width:10px;
17.  border-style:  ridge;
18.  width: 150px;}
19.  -->
20.  </style> <html> <head>
21.  <title> Interactive Resizing</title>
22.  </head>
23.  <body><div>
24.  <form  action"">
25.  Enter width:<input  type="text"  NAME="Width"  value=""><br>
26.  Enter height:<input  type="text" NAME="Height"  value=""><br>
27.  <input  type="button"  value="Resize It"  name="But1"  onclick="return ResizeIt()">
28.  </form></div>
29.  </body>
30.  </html>
```

getElementById

The method **document.getelementById()** makes searching for the exact element easy. First you must create an element ID then call the element_ID anywhere you desire. For example: <dive id="text">
var text=document.getElementById("text");
The example below changes colors by using the **getElementById()** method.

Example: 12.9

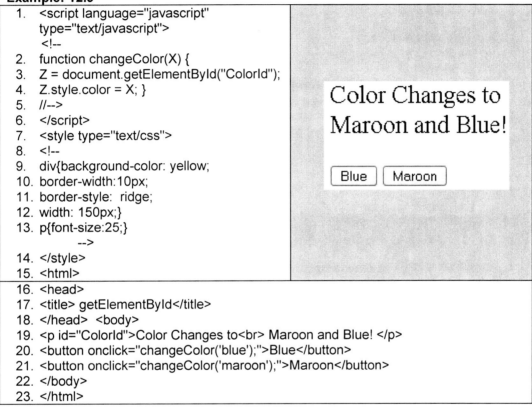

```
1.  <script language="javascript"
    type="text/javascript">
    <!--
2.  function changeColor(X) {
3.  Z = document.getElementById("ColorId");
4.  Z.style.color = X; }
5.  //-->
6.  </script>
7.  <style type="text/css">
8.  <!--
9.  div{background-color: yellow;
10. border-width:10px;
11. border-style:  ridge;
12. width: 150px;}
13. p{font-size:25;}
        -->
14. </style>
15. <html>
16. <head>
17. <title> getElementById</title>
18. </head>  <body>
19. <p id="ColorId">Color Changes to<br> Maroon and Blue! </p>
20. <button onclick="changeColor('blue');">Blue</button>
21. <button onclick="changeColor('maroon');">Maroon</button>
22. </body>
23. </html>
```

Popup window

Some time you may want to create a popup window. The Popup window is a relatively small new window that automatically loads when you visit the website. The popup always contains some message. For example sometimes when you visit an e-commerce website, a popup window automatically pops up which says,"For three days there will be 20% discount!".
Save this file as **Popy.html**

Example: 12.10

```
1.   <style type="text/css">
2.   <!--
3.   body{background-color:#d8da3d;
4.   color:maroon;
5.   text-align: center ;
6.   border-width:5px;
7.   border-style:  ridge;
8.   width: 320px;}
9.   -->
10.  </style> <html> <head>
11.  <title> Popup Window</title>
12.  </head> <body>
13.  This popup window is the new one! You can click on the button[close] to close the
     window. We use attributes like:
14.  menubar=no,resizable=no,scrollbars=no,
     width=350,height=200,toolbar=no,status=1<br><br>
15.  <input type="button" name= "bt1" value="Close"
     onclick="javascript:self.close()"></a>
16.  </body>
17.  </html>
```

The above file is just designed popup window. Now run the file below:
This program read the HTML file of **Popy.html**

```
1.   <SCRIPT TYPE='text/javascript'>
2.   <!--
3.   function popup(){
4.   window.open("Popy.html","","menubar=no,resizable=no,scrollbars=no,
     width=350,height=200,toolbar=no,status=1"); }
5.   -->
6.   </SCRIPT>
7.   <html> <head>
8.   <title>JavaScript Popup</title>
9.   </head> <body>
10.  <a href="javascript:popup();">Generate Popup</a>
11.  </body>
12.  </html>
```

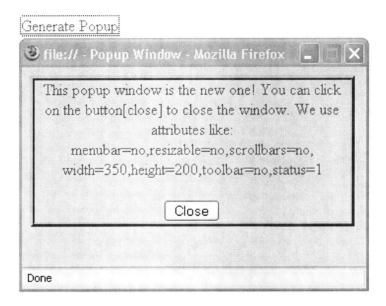

If you want the popup window to be displayed onscreen automatically, then call the **popup()** function and use the **onLoad()** function.

```
<body onload="popup()">
</body>
```

User browser information
You can write JavaScript to identify the user's browser information. For example what type of browser is the user using (NS or IE)?
Look at this table:

Property	Description
appCodeName	The code name of the browser.
appName	Browser's name
appVersion	Browser's version
cookieEnabled	Is cookie enable
language	Browser default language
platform[]	The platform of the client
plugins	Currently installed plug-ins
systemLanguage	The default language of the Operating system
userAgent	String passed by browser
userLanguage	The preferred language setting of the user

Example: 12.11

```
1.   <script type="text/javascript">
2.   <!--
3.   function Navigator(){
4.   var nav = navigator;
5.   var output="";
6.   output+=" Code Name is: "+nav.appCodeName+"\r\n";
7.   output+=" Version is: "+nav.appVersion+"\r\n";
8.   output+=" Name is: "+nav.appName+"\r\n";
9.   output+=" Cookie is: "+nav.cookieEnabled +"\r\n";
10.  output+=" Platform is: "+nav.platform+"\r\n";
11.  alert(output);
12.  }
13.  -->
14.  </script>
15.  <html>
16.  <head> <title> Browser Identification </title>
17.  <body onload=Navigator()>
18.  </body>
19.  </html>
```

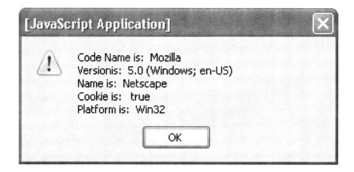

Cookies

In the above example we use the **cookieEnabled** property, now let's see what a cookie is? A cookie is a small text file that will be saved on your computer hard-disk when you visit a certain website. In fact, a cookie itself is harmless and does not pose any problem to your system. Usually cookies are written to keep track of visitors. In the Firefox browser you can see cookies under **Tool->Option-> Privacy-> Show Cookies**. From here you can delete cookies.
In Internet Explorer you can see them under
C:\Documents and Settings\YourUserName\Cookies

Saving cookies

To create a cookie we use the **setCookie()** method and we save the values of the cookie. It takes arguments like name, values and expiration.

- The name is the cookie's name.
- The value is the value of cookie (information you want the cookie to save).
- The expiration means the date that the cookie expires (duration that the cookie stays in your system).

setCookie(name, values, expiryDate)

```
<script type="text/javascript" >
<!--
SetCookie('Target', 'I am here!', 30);
 -->
</script>
```

If you use SetCookie('Target', 'I am here!'); then the expiry date ends when the browser is closed. As soon as the browser leaves the screen, this cookie will no longer exist. Cookie values cannot accept semicolons, commas, or white-space, therefore use the **escape()** method; the opposite escape method is the **unescape()** method.

Now we create a cookie that will be saved in your cookies folder.

Example: 12.12

```
1.   <script type="text/javascript">
2.   <!--
3.   function SaveCookie()
4.   {
5.   var name = document.CookieForm.textbox1.value;
6.   document.cookie = "CookieNmaes=" + name;
7.   }
8.   -->
9.   </script>
10.  <html>
11.  <head><title> JavaScript Cookie </title> </head>
12.  <body>
13.  <form action="" name="CookieForm">
14.  Enter your name:
15.  <input type="TEXT" name="textbox1">
16.  <input type="BUTTON" value="Save Cookie" onClick="SaveCookie()" >
17.  </form>
18.  </body>
19.  </html>
```

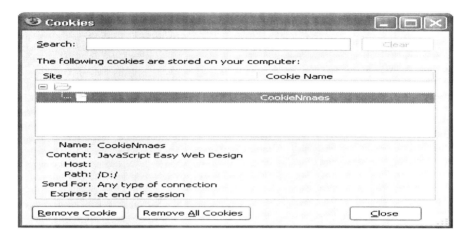

Review questions

1. What is an event?
2. onLoad event
3. onClick event
4. onFocus event
5. onBlur event
6. onMouseOver
7. onMouseOut
8. How do you prevent a window from resizing?
9. What is the _blank?
10. **window.resizeTo(x,y)**
11. **window.resizeBy(x,y)**
12. What does this property do? getElementById
13. What is appName?
14. What is appVersion?
15. What is a cookie?

Answer

1-Events are small methods that are usually placed into the HTML part and they trigger the JavaScript method.

2- Load when the page is loading

3-Waiting for user click

4-Cursor will be automatically on the focus area

5-The opacity is minimized

6-When mouse is over object

7-When a mouse gets out of object area

8-Set the Resizable=yes

9-Opens a window

10- Resizes window to specified X,Y

11- Resizes window by specified amount and grows relative to the base

12- The method document.getelementById() makes searching for the exact element easy.

13- Browser's name

14- Browser's version

15-Cookies are small text files that will be placed on the user's hard drive upon visiting some websites

Chapter 13

Multimedia and Animations

Introduction

What is multimedia? Multimedia refers to multiple communications: videos, sounds, texts, animated graphics and images delivered via communication lines or electronic devices. Multimedia is all about communicating in many different ways. As technology progresses, multimedia has grown to be part of modern communication. Everyone wants to see some sort of multimedia, such as video clips or music, embedded in the website. You can create animation with JavaScript without using graphics such as Flash or Golive and the like. JavaScript provides the way that you need to use in order to manipulate the images, videos and sounds.

Working with images

HTML has the capability to embed audio, video, simple images or animated graphics through the <embed> tag. However, the standard tag is **<object>**.

> ▐▶ **Note:** The <embed> tag has been outmoded (meaning it is no longer used) in favor of <object> tag. In fact, the <object> tag acts as multipurpose in HTML. Object refers to all the elements which have to be embedded in the HTML code.

Embedding an image

An image can be loaded along with the HTML page. It can be done by using **img** and a source tag like this: <img src=file.jpg>. You can use some attributes to identify the size of the image.
<img src="PicFile.gif" width="150" height="60">

From a website or *different location, for example*:
<img src="http://www.shanbedi.com/folder/image.jpg">

You can add a tool tip:
<img src="Cat.jpg" alt="This is Persian cat!">

Image formats

There are several image formats identified by extensions such as (**.gif**) or (**.jpg**). These four formatted images are used most often with today's Internet, and all browsers handle them well:

- **GIF**
- **JPEG or JPG**
- **PNG**
- **BMP**

Extension	Name	Description
.gif	Graphics Interchange Format	This graphics file format was used by *CompuServe* in the late 1980s. GIF supports 256 color monitors. This image is easily used in WWW.
.jpg or **.jpeg**	Joint Photographic Experts Group	JPEG is used for color images and is especially used for photos and scanning. The jpg size is smaller compared to the gif. It is familiar to most browsers.
.png	Portable Network Graphics	This new graphics format is similar to the GIF. It is designed to replace the gif. Presently all browsers handle it well.
.bmp	BitMaPped graphic	This graphics format is used in Windows. It can be created simply with MS-paint. We usually do not use .bmp on an image for the Internet. However, some parts like counters are in the .bmp format.

Simple image adding

To attach an image to your website you may use an img tag. For example: <img src="pic2.jpg">. Pic2.jpg is the file name in your working folder.

Example: 13.1
<html>
<head>
<title>HTML loading image</title>
</head>
<body bgcolor="yellow">
<img src="Hassan2.jpg" width=300 height=250>
</body>
</html>

The above program is just an image loaded with HTML. So, now we must use a JavaScript predefined function to load our images. In the previous chapter we worked with two JavaScript functions like **MouseOver()** and **MouseOut()**, here we will use the same example to refresh our memory.

Example: 13.2

```
1.    <script type="text/javascript">
2.    <!--
3.    function MouseOver() {
4.    document.Mouse.src ="MouseOver.jpg";
5.    }
6.    function MouseOut() {
7.    document.Mouse.src ="MouseOut.jpg";
8.    }
9.    -->
10. </script>
11. <html>
12. <head>
13. <title> onFocus and onBlur</title>
14. </head>
15. <body><div>
16. <a href="#" target="_blank"
17. onmouseover ="MouseOver() " onmouseout="MouseOut() ">
18. <img border="0" alt="Mouse Events!" src="MouseOut.jpg" name="Mouse"></a>
19. </div></body></html>
```

Image map

Image map is one of the most interesting and amazing parts of HTML and JavaScript. Simply put, the image map is one image with multiple clickable areas. How is this possible? First you have to have a good image with distinct regions. You must also calculate the coordinates for each region on the image (mapping). The target must be clearly identified.

Image Shapes

You can play with three different shapes:

Rect: rectangular shapes calculate top-right, bottom-left.

Circle: circular format; you need to calculate the center of a circle(X,Y) and radius (half of diameter).

Polygon: polygon shapes (many shapes); you need to calculate coordinates carefully.

Map name

In order to avoid confusion when using several maps, you need to name them properly. For example:

```
<IMG SRC="Toyota.gif" USEMAP="#Car1">
<IMG SRC="BMW.gif" USEMAP="#Car2">
<map name="Car1">
The related code!
</map>
<map name="Car2">
The related code!
</map>
```

Map target

To complete mapping the regions, you need to use some HTML keywords: "**area**", "**shape**", "**usemap**" and "**coordes**", along with the related **link**.

Example: 13.3

```
1.   <script type="text/javascript">
2.   <!--
3.   function Show(area) {
4.   alert(area);
5.   }
6.   -->
7.   </script>
8.   <html>
9.   <head>
10.  <title>JavaScript Image
     Map</title>
11.  </head>
12.  <body>
13.  <img src="Mapping1.jpg" border=0 usemap="#map">
14.  <map name=map>
```

You can download the above image from:
Http://www.shanbedi.com/Mapping1.jpg

15. <area shape="circle" coords="91,19,10" href="http://www.shanbedi.com">
16. <area shape="rect" coords="6,7,61,34" href="javascript:Show('This is a Rectangle');">
17. <area shape="default" href="javascript:Show('Here is Outside of the Shape');">
18. </map>
19. </body>
20. </html>

The above image is only one image that is divided into two parts: a *circle* and a rectangle shape. By clicking on the circle, you will see a website and by clicking on the rectangle, you will see an alert box. If you click anywhere outside of the shapes the message box shows" *Here is Outside of the Shape"*.

When a user clicks on the rectangular then the message displays, "This is a Rectangle".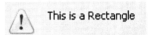

When a user clicks outside of the shapes then the message displays, "Here is outside of the Shape".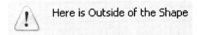

We use an attribute such as **usemap** in order to assign it to the name tag later. The above example works perfectly.

▶ **Note: javascript:Show** is inline script, which means you can use JavaScript for only a line rather than the entire code.
▶ **Wait a minute**, how did you calculate the exact coordinates?
Well, you can open your image in any image editor and it will show the coordinates. Here, we made this simple image in Photoshop and it gave us the exact coordinates.

For a rectangle, you just need to type the number of the top-right and the number of the bottom-left (4 points). For example (5,5 100,100).
For a circle, you need the two points **X, Y** and the **radius** of the clickable object.

Slide shows
A slide show can be manually or automatically operated. In case of a manual change, the user clicks on the button and sees the images one by one. It can also use an option box (combo boxes) to select a name and see the related picture. In case of an automatic (animation) change the images will be displayed slide after slide automatically. Here we look at a manual change.

Example: 13.4
```
1.  <script type="text/javascript">
2.  <!--
3.  var arr = new Array("dog1.jpg", "dog2.jpg", "dog3.jpg" );
4.  var Pic = 0;
```

```
5.   function Last() {
6.   if (document.images && Pic > 0) {
7.   Pic--;
8.   document.ShowPic.src = arr[Pic]; }
9.   }
10.  function Next() {
11.  if (document.images && Pic < 2) {
12.  Pic++;
13.  document.ShowPic.src = arr[Pic]; }
14.  }
15.  -->
16.  </script>
17.  <html>
18.  <head><Title> Slide show one by one!</title>
19.  </head>
20.  <body>
21.  <IMG SRC= "dog1.jpg" width=120 name="ShowPic"><br>
22.  <A href="javascript:Last()">[Previous]</A>
23.  <A href="javascript:Next()">[Next]</A>
24.  </body>
25.  </html>
```

[Previous] [Next]

Click on the buttons to show images one by one!

> ► **Note**: All image files are placed into an array which contains indexes from 0 to 2 (the third image index=2) There are two functions; the next contains **Pic++**, which means it goes to the next index of the array. The Last function has **Pic - -**, which means it goes back to the previous picture.

You can use buttons like arrow left and arrow right to see the sides.

**<A href="javascript:Last()"> <IMG SRC=
"ArrowLeft.jpg" ALT="Previous"> </A>
   **

**<A href="javascript:Next()"><IMG SRC=
"ArrowRight.jpg" ALT="Next"></A>**

Animation

Instead of showing slides manually you can use some loops along with an array to create animation. It automatically changes slide by slide. Once it has shown the stream of slides it automatically returns to start again from beginning. It is also interesting to see all images in a random order.

Example: 13.5

```
1. <!DOCTYPE HTML PUBLIC "-//W3C//DTD HTML 4.01 Transitional//EN"
   "http://www.w3.org/TR/html4/loose.dtd">
2. <html>
3. <head>
4. <title> Animation </title>
5. <meta http-equiv="Content-Type" content="text/html; charset=iso-8859-1">
6. <script language="JavaScript" type="text/javascript">
7. <!--
8. Dog = new Array();
9. Dog[0]= "dog1.jpg";
10. Dog[1]= "dog2.jpg";
11. Dog[2]= "dog3.jpg";
12. Dog[3]= "dog4.jpg";
13. var i = 0;
14. function showSlides(){
15. setInterval("change()", 1000);
16. }
17. function change(){
18. document.images.pics.src = Dog[i];
19. i = i + 1;
20. if (i > (Dog.length-1)) {i=0;}
21. }
22. -->
23. </script>
24. <style type="text/css">
25. <!--
26. body{background-color: yellow;
27. color: blue;
28. border-style: solid dotted;
29. width: 150px;}
30. -->
31. </style>
32. </head>
33. <body onLoad="showSlides()">
34. <div align="center">
35. <img src="dog1.jpg" name="pics" width
   ="150"> </div>
36. </body>
37. </html>
```

We use CSS, HTML and JavaScript all together. You can look at the application of the array system.

Play sounds

JavaScript provides an easy way to play sound, whether automatically or by clicking on a button.
 First you have to have a sound file in your computer (download a file and save it on your disk). Then you must call this file through the HTML embedding format. There are almost three ways to add sound (audio) to your website or your page.
The three formatted tags, **<object>**, **<embed>** and **<bgsound>**, help you to add sounds. The sound file may have an extension, such as **.wav, .mid, .mp3** or **.au**, but these four extensions are the more popular and useable in today's multimedia programs. Let's first use the embed tag to add sound on our page.
<embed src="filename.wav" width=" xx " height="xx" autoplay="false" hidden="false" loop="false" volume="xx"></embed>
If **autopaly** is set to true then it automatically starts.
If you set **hidden=true** then the box will not be shown.
If **loop** is set to true then it will be looped.
Volume can be from 1 to 100. By default it is set to 50.

In addition you can use the **direct link** like:
<A HREF="http://www.mydomain.com/sounds/soundfile.mid">Listen to song</A>

There has always been a problem regarding embedding sound into the website.
The <**bgsound**>tag is not a valid HTML or XHTML tag but works in IE
The <**embed**> tag is not a valid HTML or XHTML tag, but it works in most browsers.
The <**object**> - tag is a valid HTML and XHTML tag, but it works in some browsers. It is the new XHTML object. The simple way to play sound with JavaScript is to create a function and call this function.

```
function PlayMusic() {
  document.Sounds.play(); }
<body>
<EMBED SRC="Cat.wav" hidden=false  autostart=false   name="Sounds">
<a href="javascript: PlayMusic() ">Play now!</a>
</body>
```

Example: 13.6

```
1.  <script type="text/javascript">
2.  <!--
3.  function PlayMusic() {
4.  if (document.embeds) {
5.  if (navigator.appName == 'Netscape')
6.  document.embeds[0].play();
7.  else
8.  document.embeds[0].run(); }
9.  }
10. //-->
11. </script>
```

12. \<html>
13. \<head>
14. \<title> Playing Sounds\</title>
15. \</head> \<body onLoad="PlayMusic();">
16. \<embed src="Dog.wav" hidden=false loop=false autostart=true>
17. \</body>
18. \</html>

The **embeds** property is an array that contains all the embedded objects and plug-in tags. It has a property "length" which starts from 0 to length -1.

Sounds with control

You can control several parts of a sound. For example: volume, stop, start, pause and so on. There are several neat functions such as **play(), stop(), pause()** and the like, which help you to manage and control sounds.

Example: 13.7

1. \<script type="text/javascript">
2. \<!--
3. function playIt() {
4. document.Sounds.play(); }
5. function pauseIt() {
6. document.Sounds.pause();
7. }
8. function StopIt() {
9. document.Sounds.stop();
10. }
11. -->
12. \</script>
13. \<html>
14. \<head>\<title>Sound In JavaScript\</title>
15. \</head>
16. \<body>
17. \<EMBED SRC="Jadval.wav" HIDDEN=false AUTOSTART=FALSE NAME="Sounds">
18. \<P>\<A href="javascript:playIt()">Play\</A>\</P>
19. \<P>\<A href="javascript:pauseIt()">Pause \</A>\</P>
20. \<P>\<A href="javascript:StopIt()">Stop \</A>\</P>
21. \</body>
22. \</html>

Play

Pause

Stop

Sounds from the website

You can listen to the sound that already exists on your server. Simply write a short program in pure HTML or JavaScript and run it. Look at this song to which you are listening directly from the website. We use the embed tag. We modify the above example to read from the website.

Example: 13.8

```
1.  <script type="text/javascript">
2.  <!--
3.  function playIt() {
4.  document.Sounds.play();
5.  }
6.  function pauseIt() {
7.  document.Sounds.pause();
8.  }
9.  function StopIt() {
10. document.Sounds.stop();
11. }
12. -->
13. </script>
14. <html>
15. <head><title>Sound In JavaScript</title>
16. </head>
17. <body>
18. <EMBED SRC='http://www.shanbedi.com/Music/Homeira.mp3' HIDDEN=false
    AUTOSTART=FALSE   NAME='Sounds'>
19. <P><A href="javascript:playIt()">Play</A></P>
20. <P><A href="javascript:pauseIt()">Pause </A></P>
21. <P><A href="javascript:StopIt()">Stop </A></P>
22. </body>
23. </html>
```

Play

Pause

Stop

Using HTML Object

Earlier we mentioned that <embed> has been abandoned in favor of the **<object>** tag, which provides more functions. Consequently, we should no longer be using <embed>.

What is wrong with <embed> tag?

As you can see, the format for the embed tag is **<embed src =" "/>** and the format for the object tag is **<object data= " " > ...</object>**.

Is there something wrong with the <embed> tag? The reality is that there are different browsers out there, each implementing HTML codes differently. The embed tag was first introduced by Netscape Navigator 2 and it has never become an HTML standard. One of the major problems is that when you leave a page and try to visit another page, it ends without user permission. This causes problems for those who may want to visit several websites or pages and listen to their favorite music.

List of some important browsers

Mozila FireFox	Mozilla is an open source project, including Firefox and Minimo Mobile Browser. It comes from the old Netscape.
Microsoft Internet Explorer (IE)	Comes from Microsoft.
Konqueror	Unix-based Web browser.
Safari	KHTML-based broser for Apple Computers and is optimized for Mac OS X.
Opera	Browser support for **BitTorrent** with multiple search engines.

Watch movie

The simple way to see a movie is to use the old code which downloads the file completely. In this way, you automatically see the video.

Example: 13.9

```
1.  <script type="text/javascript">
2.  <!--
3.  function playIt() {
4.  document.Sounds.play();
5.  }
6.  function pauseIt() {
7.  document.Sounds.pause();
8.  }
9.  function StopIt() {
10. document.Sounds.stop();
11. }
12. -->
13. </script>

14. <html>
15. <head><title>Sound In JavaScript</title>
16. </head> <body>
17. <EMBED SRC='http://www.shanbedi.com/Music/Shebo.wmv' HIDDEN=false
        AUTOSTART=FALSE   NAME = 'Sounds'>
18. <P><A href="javascript:playIt()">Play</A></P>
19. <P><A href="javascript:pauseIt()">Pause </A></P>
20. <P><A href="javascript:StopIt()">Stop </A></P>
21. </body>
22. </html>
```

Adding an applet animation

It is simple to add an applet (java) *animation* or image to the website. You must add the compiled object of the applet, which is a "class" extension. You simply write a code like:
*<Applet Code="**AppletFile.class**" width=300 Height=300>*
</Applet>

JavaScript menus

In fact, most parts of a menu are related to the design. As we mentioned throughout the book HTML is all about contents, CSS is a way to design and JavaScript is a way to create dynamic pages. You see we use the combination of all three, which is sometimes called DHTML. In order to create more menus look at the CSS part of this book. Here we just bring a simple hover menu with CSS and JavaScript.

Example: 13.10

1.   <style type="text/css">
2.   #menu {
3.   border: 5px ridge yellow;
4.   width: 180px;
5.   background-color: #d8da3d;}
6.   #menu a {
7.   display: block;
8.   font: bold 14px Arial;
9.   padding: 2px;
10.   padding-left: 5px;
11.   color: blue;
12.   text-decoration: none;
13.   border-bottom: 1px ridge black; }
14.   #menu a:hover{
15.   background-color: blue;
16.   color: black; }
17.   </style>
18.   <html>
19.   <head><title> Hover menu </title> </head>
20.   <body>
21.   <div id="menu">
22.   <a href="#">JavaScript</a>
23.   <a href="#">PHP Web Design</a>
24.   <a href="#">CSS Web Design</a>
25.   <a href="#">XHTML Web Design</a>
26.   <a href="#">DHTML Web Design</a>
27.   </div>
28.   </body>
29.   </html>

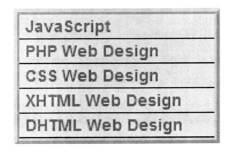

When you put the mouse over the button background and text will be changed.

DOM

DOM (**D**ocument **O**bject **M**odel) allows a JavaScript programmer to manipulate data, and to add and delete documents. This diagram shows what the DOM is:

- ▶ **Window:** Frame, History, Location and Document
- ▶ **Document:** Link, Image, Area, Applet, Form
- ▶ **Form:** Text, password, Hidden, Radio, submit, Reset, FileUpload, CheckBox, Button, Select (option)
- ▶ **Navigator:** Plugin

NOTE: The **DOM** is covered throughout this book.

DHTML

What is DHTML? The **DTML** is means Dynamic-HTML and more precisely refers to the combination of HTML contents, CSS styles and JavaScript dynamic pages.

NOTE: DHTML is covered in this book without mentioning its name.

Review questions

1. The embed tag has been abandoned in favor of_____
2. What is wrong with this tag?
   <img src "PicFile.gif" width="150" height="60">
3. Which of these extensions are not image formats?
   - **GIFS**
   - **JPG**
   - **PNGI**
   - **BMP**
4. MouseOver() and MouseOut() are both the same   True   False
5. What is the image map?
6. What does this code means in the slide show?
   if (document.images && Pic > 0) {
   Pic--;
   document.ShowPic.src = arr[Pic]; }
7. Can we use arrays and loops to create an animation? Yes   No
8. What happens If **autopaly** is set to true?
9. This code attaches an applet to your website True   False
   *<Applet Code="**AppletFile.class**" width=300 Height=300> </Applet>*
10. What is DHTML?

Answer

1. The object tag
2. The correct version is:
   <img src = "PicFile.gif" width="150" height="60">
3. GIFS and PNGI
4. False
5. An image map divides an image into several clickable regions
6. When there are more images then it goes back one by one
7. Yes
8. If **autopaly** is set to true then it plays music without user permission
9. True
10. DHTML is a combination of HTML, CSS and JavaScript

Laboratory exercises

1- Download an image of a Canadian map and then map it to at least 4 provinces. When you click on BC, it will display the BC provincial map or if you click on Ontario, it will display the map of Ontario.
2- Write a code that embeds a video. For the purpose of IE, use the <object> tag. You may want to have access to the video by using the website.
3- Download an applet animation from a free site and then attach it to the website.
4- Create a menu which upon a *mouseover* command displays a submenu.

Appendix

Font groups in CSS

CSS Font size groups			
Length group	**Absolute group**	**Relative group**	**Percentage group**
font-size: normal font-size:10px font-size:12pt	font-size:x-small font-size:xx-small font-size:small font-size:medium font-size:large font-size:x-large font-size:xx-large	font-size:smaller font-size:larger	font-size:50%

pt (points; 1pt=1/72in)
pc (picas; 1pc=12pt)
em (the height of the element's font)
px (pixels)
Please note, "pt" is a print unit, and not a exact screen unit.
Fonts can be manipulated by these features: font-size, font-style, font-variant, font-weight, line-height, and font-family.

HTML entities

HTML Entities			
Character	**Entity**	**Decimal**	**Result**
quotation mark	&quot;	&#34;	"
ampersand	&amp;	&#38;	&
less-than sign	&lt;	&#60;	<
greater-than sign	&gt;	&#62;	>
euro sign	&euro;	&#8364;	€
copyright sign	&copy;	&#169;	©

Image extensions

Extension	Name	Description
.gif	Graphics Interchange Format	This graphics file format used by the CompuServe in the late 1980. GIF supports 256 color monitors. I this an easy image to be used in WWW.
.jpg or **.jpeg**	Joint Photographic Experts Group	Data compression for color images especially used for photos and scanning. The jpg size is smaller compare to gif. It is familiar for most browsers.
.png	Portable Network Graphics	This new graphics format is similar to the GIF. It designed to be replacing to the gif. Presently all browsers are handling it well.
.bmp	BitMaPped graphic	This graphics format used in the Windows. It can be simply created by MS-paint. We usually do not use .bmp on image for internet but some parts like counter is in bmp format.

List of some important browsers

Mozila FireFox	Mozilla is an open source projects, including Firefox, Minimo Mobile Browser. It comes from old Netscape.
Microsoft Internet Explorer (IE)	Come from Microsoft
Konqueror	Unix-based Web browser
Safari	KHTML-based web for Apple Computers and optimized for Mac OS X.
Opera	Browser support for **BitTorren**t, with multiple search engines.

Declaration of selector

Selector	Property	Value
P	{ color :	blue ; }

Fonts Property

Property	Example
font-family	font-family : arial, san-serif
font-size	font-size: normal font-size:10px (pixel size) font-size:12pt (point size) **Relative size :** font-size:small font-size:x-small font-size:xx-small font-size:smaller font-size:medium font-size:large font-size:x-large font-size:xx-large font-size:larger font-size:55%
font-style	font-style:normal font-style:italic font-style:oblique
font-weight	font-weight:normal font-weight:bold font-weight:bolder font-weight:lighter **font-weight:100**
• If the font-family made up of two parts like Arial narrow then you should place it into quotation like: font-family: "Arial narrow". • The font-weight can be between 100 to 900. • Normal=400 and bold=700	

Color Text & Backgrounds

To color text background:	**div.textBack1 { background-color: gray; }**
Text foreground:	**div.textColor{ color: " #0000ff " }**
You can use the RGB value:	**div.textColor{ color:rgb(0 0 255) }**
To color page background:	**body { background-color: yellow; }**

Border property

Properties	Values	Example
border-bottom-width **border-left-width** **border-width** **border-top-width** **border-right-width**	thin , medium , thick, length	border-bottom-width: thin
border-top-color **border-right-color** **border-bottom-color** **border-left-color** **border-color**	Any color, Use rgb, color name or hexadecimal value	border-right-color : blue or border-bottom-color : #CCCCCC
border-bottom-style **border-left-style** **border-style** **border-top-style** **border-right-style**	none , solid , double , groove , ridge , inset , outset You can use combination of both like: solid double or bauble solid.	border-right-style: groove border-style: dotted border-style: hidden border-style: solid
border-top **border-right** **border-bottom** **border-left** **border**	*border-width, border-style,* *border-color*	border-bottom: thick inset yellow

Text properties

Properties	Value	Example
letter-spacing	normal , *length*	**letter-spacing:4pt**
vertical-align	sub , super	**vertical-align:sub**
text-decoration	none , underline, overline , line-through	**text-decoration:none**
text-transform	capitalize , uppercase , lowercase , none	**text-transform: lowercase**
text-align	left , right , center , justify	**text-align: center**
text-indent	*length* , *percentage*	**text-indent:10px**
line-height	normal , *number* , *length* , *percentage*	**line-height:normal**
white-space	normal ,pre, nowrap	**White-space:normal**

List Properties

Property	Value	Example
list-style-position	inside outside	**ol { list-style-position:inside; }** **ul { list-style-position:outside;** **}**
list-style-image	URL	**ul { list-style-image:url(image1.jpg); }**
list-style	Can declare multiple attributes list-style-type list-style-position list-style-image	**ul { list-style:disc inside url(image.gif); }**
marker-offset	auto	**ol:before { display:marker; marker-offset:3px; }**
list-style-type	disc circle square decimal decimal-leading-zero lower-roman upper-roman lower-alpha upper-alpha lower-greek lower-latin upper-latin hebrew armenian georgian cjk-ideographic hiragana katakana hiragana-iroha katakana-iroha	**ol { list-style-type: lower-latin; }** **ul { list-style-type:circle; }**

Table Properties in CSS

Property	Value
border-collapse	collapse separate
border-spacing	length length
caption-side	top bottom left right

empty-cell	show hide
table-layout	auto fixed

Links:
A:link is used for a new link.
A:visited is used for visited link.
A:active is used for activate the link when you click on it.
A:hover is used for mouse over the link (e.g. changes color).

Text decorations
text-decoration:none means no decoration around the selected text
text-decoration:underline return a underline bar
text-decoration:overline return an over line bar
text-decoration:line-through return a bar through the text
text-decoration:blink return blinking but does not work under IE

Margin properties

Margin Properties		
Properties	**Value**	**Example**
margin-top		margin-top:5px
margin-bottom		margin-bottom:5em
margin-left	*length* , *percentage* , auto	margin-left:5pt
margin-right		margin-right:5px
margin		margin: 15px 5px 10px 15px

Overflow

Overflow properties	
Visible	default
Hidden	Does not display scrollbar
Auto	Automatic display of scroll when text is large
Scroll	Display scrollbar

Filter effects

Filter name	Effect
Filter: alpha	Create opacity that becomes light by the end
Filter: blur	Creates blur object
Filter: chroma	Works with image, makes transparent
Filter: dropshadow	Create dropping shadow along X and y with specified color

Filter: glow	Creates some glows around the object
Filter: shadow	Something between *dropshadow* and glow
Filter: flipH	Flipping horizontally
Filter: flipV	Flipping vertically
Filter: grayscale	Convert color to shaded gray
Filter: wave	Creates wave shape of an object
Filter: xray	Grayscale color kind of x-ray image
Filter: invert	Create the negative or opposite site of the color number
Filter: mask	Shift transparent to specified color

Escape Sequence

Escape Sequence	Character
\'	Single quotation mark
\"	Double quotation mark
\\	Backslash
\b	Backspace
\f	Form feed
\n	New line
\r	Carriage return
\t	Tab
\ddd	ddd Octal sequence
\xdd	Hexadecimal sequence

Mathematical Operator		
Operator	Name	Example
+	Addition	A = B + C
-	Subtraction	A = B - C
*	Multiplication	A = B * C
/	Division	A = B / C
%	Modulus	A = B % C
++	Increment	A = B + +
--	Decrement	A = B --

Logical Operators

Type	Symbol	Example
AND	&&	((2<3)&&(4>5)) false, two sides must be true
OR	||	((2<3)||(4>5)) true, one sides must be true
NOT	!	If(!A>100)

» **getDate()**   Day of the month (0-31)
» **getTime()**   Number of milliseconds since 1/1/1970 at 12:00 AM
» **getSeconds()**   Number of seconds (0-59)
» **getMinutes()**   Number of minutes (0-59)
» **getHours()**   Number of hours (0-23)
» **getDay()**   Day of the week(0-6) where 0 = Sunday, ... and 6 = Saturday
» **getMonth()**   Number of month (0-11)
» **getFullYear()** The four digit year (1970-9999)

Date and Time

Letter	Description
d	Day of the month as one digits(single digit)
dd	Day of the month as two digits(leading zero)
ddd	Day in three-letter abbreviation
dddd	Day in full name
m	Month as a digits
mm	Month of the month as two digits(leading zero)
mmm	Month with three-letter abbreviation
mmmm	Month in full name
yy	Year as last two digits, leading zero
yyyy	Year as four digits.
h	Hours with no leading zero in a single-digit (12-hour clock)
hh	Hours with leading zero in a single-digit (12-hour clock)
H	Hours with no leading zero in a single-digit (24-hour clock)
HH	Hours with leading zero in a single-digit (24-hour clock)
M	Minutes with no leading zero in a single-digit
MM	Minutes with leading zero in a single-digit
s	Seconds with no leading zero in a single-digit
ss	Seconds with leading zero in a single-digit

Method	Description
anchor()	To create an HTML anchor
big()	Big text size
blink()	String blinking
bold()	Bold string
charAt()	Returns the character at a defined position, charAt(10)
charCodeAt()	Returns the Unicode character at a defined position
concat()	Concatenating strings
fixed()	Displays a string as teletype text

fontcolor()	Color string
fontsize()	String font size
indexOf()	Index of specified value
italics()	Italic text
lastIndexOf()	Last part of index
link()	String as a hyperlink
match()	Searches in a string
replace()	Replaces specified characters with some other characters
search()	Searches for values in a string
slice()	Slicing string
small()	Small font
split()	Splits a string into an array of strings
strike()	In a strike format
sub()	Subscript
substr()	A specified number of characters in a string
substring()	Characters in a string between two specified indices
sup()	Superscript
toLowerCase()	Return to lowercase letters
toUpperCase()	Return to uppercase letters
toSource()	The source code of an string object
valueOf()	The primitive value of a String object

JavaScript Events

Event name	Description
onAbort	Aborts an image from loading
onFocus	Focuses on the text box
onChange	Data will be changed by user
onClick	Waiting for user click
onDblClick	Acts when user clicks twice
onDragDrop	An icon is dragged and dropped into the browser
onError	Acts usually when JavaScript error occurs
onBlur	Reverse of the focus, loses focus
onKeyDown	User press a key
onKeyPress	Acts when a user presses or holds down a key.
onKeyUp	Acts when a user releases a key.
onLoad	Automatically load acts when page loads
onMouseDown	Acts when user presses a mouse button.
onMouseMove	Acts when user moves the mouse.
onMouseOut	Acts when mouse leaves the button
onMouseOver	Acts when mouse is placed on the button(without clicking)
onMouseUp	Acts when user releases a mouse button.
onMove	Acts when user moves a window frame.

onReset	Clear all boxes
onResize	Allows a user to resize window or window frame.
onSelect	Allows a user to select text within the field.
onSubmit	Acts when user presses submit
onUnload	Acts when user leaves the page

- **window.location.reload()** //reloads window
- **window.close()** //closes window
- **window.moveTo(x,y)** //moves window to exact specified location
- **window.moveBy(x,y)** // move by a specified distance from their current location.
- **window.resizeTo(x,y)** //resizes window to specified X,Y
- **window.resizeBy(x,y)** //resizes window by specified shrink and grow relative to original window.

Index

Printed in the United States
132634LV00005B/36/P